RECLAIM YOUR SELF-ESTEEM

Strategies to Heal Rejection, Rebuild Self Worth and Resilience

By

Carol Moore

Table of Content

Introduction

"Out of suffering have emerged the strongest souls; the most massive characters are seared with scars." – Khalil Gibran.

Rejection activates the same parts of your brain as physical pain, and studies show it can even temporarily lower your IQ. This startling fact underscores how deeply rejection impacts our mental and physical well-being. The experience of rejection isn't just an emotional blow; it triggers a biological response, making your brain feel as though you are in physical pain. This can affect your cognitive functions, making it harder to think clearly and make decisions.

Imagine being told by someone you love that they no longer care for you. The emotional and physical pain can be overwhelming, leaving you feeling lost and broken. This kind of rejection can shatter your sense of self and leave you questioning your worth. You might find yourself replaying every moment, trying to understand what went wrong, and wondering if you'll ever feel whole again.

Why does rejection hurt so deeply, and how can you overcome it to find happiness again? The pain of rejection stems from our biological makeup and emotional connections. When faced with rejection, you may feel isolated and disconnected, as if a part of you is missing. The key to recovery lies in understanding these effects and rebuilding your self-esteem and resilience.

Chances are you picked up this book because you're dealing with the sting of rejection and seeking a way to heal. Whether it's a breakup, a friendship that ended abruptly, or being passed over for a job you desperately wanted, rejection leaves a deep mark. You may feel a mix of emotions—**sadness, anger, confusion, and even fear.** The nights can be especially tough, with your mind racing and sleep feeling like an impossible dream. Maybe you've noticed changes in your appetite or find it hard to focus at work. Each of these scenarios is a testament to the pervasive impact of rejection, but the fact that you're here means you're ready to take the first step toward healing.

This book aims to provide you with a comprehensive guide to understanding, healing from, and ultimately overcoming rejection. You will learn about the emotional and physical effects of rejection, practical steps to rebuild your self-worth, and strategies to develop resilience.

I have spent over 30 years as a psychologist and psychotherapist, helping individuals cope with and overcome several psychological traumas. Throughout my career, I've seen firsthand how devastating rejection can be and witnessed incredible transformations. My clients have taught me that while rejection is incredibly painful, it is also a powerful catalyst for growth. In this book, I will share insights from my professional experience, offering you tools and techniques that have helped countless others. My goal is to help you see that your pain has a solution, and that you can emerge from this experience stronger and more resilient.

The structure of this book is designed to be straightforward and easy to navigate. Each chapter builds on the previous one, providing a step-by-step approach to understanding and overcoming rejection. You will find practical advice, exercises, and real-life examples to help you along the way.

As you read, I encourage you to take notes and reflect on your personal experiences. Use the journaling prompts and exercises to delve deeper into your emotions and track your progress. Healing from rejection is a personal journey, and your active participation will enhance your recovery.

Remember, this is about you and your growth. Take your time, be kind to yourself, and know that healing is possible. Each step you take brings you closer to reclaiming your self-esteem and building a more resilient, happier you. Embrace this process with an open heart, and trust that better days are ahead.

Happy reading!

***

PART 1

Understanding Rejection

Chapter 1: The Nature of Rejection

"Success is not final, failure is not fatal: It is the courage to continue that counts." – Winston Churchill.

Before we can move forward, let's take a moment to understand what rejection truly is. Imagine a moment when you felt left out, excluded, or simply turned down. It stings, doesn't it? Rejection is that feeling of being dismissed or unappreciated by others, and it's something that everyone experiences at some point in their life—no matter your age, gender, or background.

Think about how rejection has shown up in your life. Maybe it was in a personal relationship where you felt overlooked, or perhaps in a professional setting where your ideas were brushed aside. These moments can be tough, right? They challenge your sense of belonging and self-worth, making you question yourself in ways you never thought possible. It's okay to admit that rejection can lead to feelings of sadness, frustration, and even self-doubt. We've all been there.

But here's the thing: you're not alone in this. Understanding the nature of rejection is the first step in learning how to navigate through it and come out stronger on the other side. Together, we'll explore how to face rejection head-on and use it as a stepping stone toward growth and self-discovery.

Types of Rejection

Rejection can occur in many different areas of life, but it primarily falls into three main categories: romantic, social, and professional. Each of these types carries its own unique challenges and emotional responses.

Romantic Rejection

- **Unrequited Love:** Unrequited love occurs when one person has strong feelings for another, but those feelings are not reciprocated. This type of rejection can be particularly painful because it often involves a deep emotional investment that goes unfulfilled. Take a moment to reflect a scenario; you have developed strong feelings for a colleague or a friend, and after mustering the courage to express your emotions, you are met with indifference or a polite refusal. The sting of this rejection can leave you questioning your attractiveness and worthiness of love.

- **Breakups:** Breakups, another common form of romantic rejection, can shatter your sense of stability and security. Whether the relationship ended due to mutual agreement or one partner's decision, the emotional fallout can be immense. You might find yourself reminiscing about the good times, wondering where things went wrong, and feeling overwhelming loss. Breakups often force you to confront the reality that a significant part of your life has changed, and you must adapt to a new normal.

- **Infidelity:** Infidelity, perhaps the most devastating form of romantic rejection, involves a partner's betrayal. Discovering that your partner has been unfaithful can be a severe blow to your self-esteem and trust. The pain of infidelity is not just about the act itself but the broken trust and the emotional connection you believed you shared. This type of rejection can lead to long-lasting emotional scars, making it difficult to trust future partners and form new relationships.

Social Rejection

- **Exclusion from Groups:** Being excluded from a social group can be incredibly isolating. Social rejection can make you feel invisible and unimportant, whether it's being left out of social gatherings, ignored by colleagues, or feeling like an outsider in your community. For example, imagine you join a new workplace and find that your colleagues have formed tight-knit groups that don't seem to welcome new members. The sense of being on the periphery can erode your confidence and make you dread social interactions.

- **Friendship Breakdowns:** Friendship breakdowns occur when close friends drift apart or have a falling out. These situations can be particularly painful because friendships often provide a vital source of support and companionship. Losing a friend can feel like losing a part of yourself, especially if the friendship was long-standing and meaningful. The emotional impact can be profound, leaving you feeling abandoned and questioning your ability to form lasting connections.

- **Bullying:** Bullying, an extreme form of social rejection, involves being targeted for harassment and exclusion by peers. Whether it happens in school, at work, or online, bullying can have devastating effects on your mental health and self-esteem. The constant barrage of negative comments and actions can make you feel helpless and unworthy, leading to anxiety, depression, and even thoughts of self-harm.

Professional Rejection

- **Job Application Rejections:** Receiving a rejection letter after applying for a job you were excited about can be disheartening. It can make you question your skills, experience, and career path. For instance, imagine you applied for your dream job, spent hours perfecting your resume and cover letter, and performed well in the interviews, only to receive a rejection email. The disappointment can be overwhelming, making you doubt your professional abilities and worth.

- **Failures in Business Ventures:** Starting a business requires significant effort, resources, and emotional investment. When a business venture fails, it can feel like a personal failure. You might question your decision-making skills, creativity, and potential for success. The financial losses and the impact on your reputation can add to the stress, making it hard to find the motivation to try again.

- **Peer Disapproval:** In the workplace, peer disapproval can manifest as not being chosen for a project, receiving negative feedback, or being overlooked for a promotion. This can undermine your confidence and job satisfaction. For example, imagine you worked hard on a project, putting in extra hours and effort, only to have your contributions dismissed by your team leader or colleagues. This type of rejection can make you feel undervalued and question your place in the professional environment.

Famous Failures: How Rejection Shaped Their Success

J.K. Rowling, the author of the Harry Potter series, faced numerous rejections from publishers before achieving monumental success. Despite these setbacks, she persevered, and her books have since sold over 500 million copies worldwide. Her story illustrates the importance of persistence and believing in your potential, even when faced with rejection.

Oprah Winfrey also faced significant rejection early in her career. She was fired from her first television job as an anchor because she was deemed "unfit for TV." Instead of letting this rejection define her, Oprah used it as a stepping stone to build an incredibly successful career. She became one of the most influential media personalities in the world, proving that rejection can be a catalyst for growth and resilience.

Everyday people also experience rejection in deeply impactful ways. You should not let rejection define you or dictate your future. Instead, use it as a stepping stone to develop resilience and find new opportunities. Many individuals who face rejection succeed by redirecting their energy and focus toward new goals.

Myths and Misconceptions

Let's take a moment to clear the air about some common misconceptions surrounding rejection. It's easy for you to fall into the trap of believing everything you hear, especially when you're feeling vulnerable after facing rejection. But here's the truth: not everything you've been told about rejection is accurate. Let's dispel some of the most prevalent myths and set the record straight.

Myth 1 – Rejection Means You're Unworthy or Flawed: This belief can lead to a cycle of self-blame and decreased self-esteem. It's crucial to understand that rejection often has more to do with the circumstances and preferences of others rather than your intrinsic value. For example, being turned down for a job might simply mean that another candidate had specific skills the employer was looking for, not that you are unqualified or incapable.

Myth 2 – Rejection is Always a Negative Experience: While rejection is undoubtedly painful, it can also serve as a powerful learning opportunity. Each rejection can teach you something about yourself, your strengths, and areas for improvement. Embracing this perspective can help you grow and develop resilience. For instance, being rejected in a romantic relationship might lead you to understand your needs better and seek more compatible partners in the future.

Myth 3 – Some People are Immune to Rejection: Some people believe that certain individuals are immune to rejection, thinking that successful or attractive people never face rejection. This is far from the truth. Everyone, regardless of their status or appearance, experiences rejection at some point in their lives. Recognizing that rejection is a universal experience can help you feel less isolated and more connected to others. Even celebrities and successful entrepreneurs face rejection regularly, but their ability to persevere and learn from these experiences sets them apart.

End of Chapter Reflection

Throughout this chapter, we've explored the nature of rejection, its various forms, and the myths and misconceptions that often surround it. Understanding these aspects is the first step toward developing a healthier perspective on rejection and finding ways to cope with its impact.

Journaling Prompts

- **Reflect on Rejection:** Describe a time when you experienced rejection. How did it make you feel, and what did you learn from the experience?

- **Challenge Beliefs:** What myths about rejection have you believed in the past? How has your perspective changed after reading this chapter?
- **Learn from Others:** Write about someone you admire who has overcome rejection. What can you learn from their experience that you can apply to your own life?
- **Identify Patterns:** Think about the patterns in your past rejections. Are there common factors or triggers? How can understanding these patterns help you in the future?
- **Self-Reflection:** How do you usually respond to rejection? Is there a way you could handle it differently to promote your emotional well-being?

In the next chapter, we will discuss why rejection hurts so much. You will explore the evolutionary reasons behind this pain, the various parts of the brain affected, and the psychological theories that explain these intense feelings.

Chapter 2: Why Rejection Hurts So Much

"Pain is inevitable, but suffering is optional." – Buddha.

Biological and Evolutionary Reasons for the Pain of Rejection

Have you ever wondered why rejection hurts so much, even when you know it's not the end of the world? It's not just in your head—there's a deeper, evolutionary reason behind it.

Let's start by thinking back to early human history. Imagine yourself as part of a small group of people, living in a time when being alone wasn't just lonely—it was dangerous. Back then, your survival depended on being part of a group. Why? Because groups offered protection from predators, access to food, and the chance to work together to meet daily challenges. If you were isolated, your chances of surviving and thriving were slim. This need for social connection has been wired into your brain over thousands of years, making rejection not just an emotional pain but a deeply rooted survival response.

Now, consider how being part of a group also played a key role in reproduction. In those early days, being accepted into a stable social group didn't just mean you were safe—it meant you had better chances of finding a mate and raising children who would survive. Within these groups, sharing resources, protecting the young, and passing on survival skills were all crucial. If you were valued by your group, you thrived, and so did your offspring. This is why the drive for social acceptance and cooperation became so deeply embedded in your nature.

This brings us to today. Even though the threats are different, your brain still reacts to rejection in a similar way. Feeling rejected triggers a primal response, almost as if your brain is sounding an alarm: "Danger! You're being pushed out of the group!" This emotional pain is your brain's way of keeping you alert and encouraging you to maintain those all-important social bonds.

This evolutionary background can help you see why rejection feels so intense. It's not just about the moment—it's about thousands of years of human history pushing you to seek connection and avoid exclusion. And that's why, even now, the need for social bonds remains a fundamental part of who you are.

How Rejection Threatens Our Need for Belonging and Security

Belonging isn't just a nice-to-have; it's a fundamental part of what makes you feel secure and valued. It's embedded in your psychological makeup, crucial to your overall well-being. **Maslow's Hierarchy of Needs** places belonging right after the basics of survival—food, water, and safety—showing just how essential it is. When you feel like you belong, you find emotional security, acceptance, and support from those around you. These connections shape your identity and boost your self-esteem. Without them, feelings of loneliness and emotional distress can creep in, leaving you feeling unanchored.

In the world we live in today, this need for belonging shows up in various aspects of your life. It's in the friendships you cherish, the family ties you maintain, and the groups or communities you're part of. The desire to be accepted and valued is something everyone shares. But when this need goes unmet—whether through exclusion from a social circle or the end of a meaningful relationship—it can shake you to your core, leaving you with a deep sense of loss and insecurity.

When you're excluded or isolated, it's not just your feelings that are affected—your brain sees it as a real threat. This sense of being cut off triggers stress responses that can lead to anxiety, depression, and a sense of worthlessness. The effects of isolation can be as harmful to your mental health as physical injury is to your body. Studies show that when social isolation drags on, it can result in severe mental health issues like chronic depression and anxiety disorders. Without social interaction, you're deprived of the emotional support and validation that help you navigate life's challenges.

Rejection doesn't just hurt—it sets off alarms in your brain, activating survival instincts that push you into stress mode. This reaction is deeply rooted in your evolutionary past (as we have discussed earlier), where staying connected to a group was a matter of life and death. When you face rejection, your brain kicks into high gear, releasing stress hormones like **cortisol**. This rush of stress is your body's way of urging you to repair those broken social bonds. But in today's world, where rejection can come in more subtle forms, this heightened stress response can spiral into chronic anxiety and emotional turmoil if not addressed.

How the Brain Processes Rejection and Emotional Pain

The anterior cingulate cortex (ACC) plays a central role in processing the emotional aspects of rejection. This brain region is involved in regulating emotional responses and detecting social pain. When you experience rejection, the ACC is activated, signaling emotional distress. This response is similar to how your brain processes physical pain, highlighting the deep-seated nature of social pain. Other brain regions also contribute to processing rejection:

Amygdala

The amygdala is responsible for emotional processing and detecting threats. When you experience rejection, the amygdala becomes active, heightening feelings of fear and anxiety. This brain region helps you react to potential dangers by triggering your body's fight or flight response. In the context of social rejection, the amygdala's activation can lead to intense emotional reactions, such as panic or overwhelming sadness, as it perceives the rejection as a threat to your social bonds and well-being.

Prefrontal Cortex

The prefrontal cortex is involved in decision-making and emotional regulation. It helps you process and cope with the emotional impact of rejection by allowing you to think rationally and manage your emotional responses. When rejection occurs, the prefrontal cortex works to assess the situation, consider the consequences, and formulate a plan for moving forward. This brain region is essential for maintaining emotional balance and preventing impulsive reactions that might worsen the situation.

Functional MRI studies have shown that these brain regions light up during experiences of social exclusion, providing a clear link between emotional pain and brain activity. These studies illustrate that the neural pathways activated during rejection are similar to those triggered by physical pain, underscoring the profound impact of social rejection on your overall well-being.

Rejection and Physical Pain

The overlap between neural pathways for physical pain and social pain explains why rejection feels so intense. Both types of pain activate similar brain regions, including the **anterior cingulate cortex.** This neural overlap means that your brain struggles to distinguish between physical and emotional pain, experiencing both with comparable intensity.

Studies have demonstrated this connection, showing that the same areas of the brain are active during physical injuries and social rejection. This finding helps explain why rejection can be so debilitating and why the pain lingers long after the initial experience.

Interestingly, research has shown that painkillers like **Tylenol** can reduce the emotional pain associated with rejection. This effect underscores the physical nature of social pain and highlights the potential for interventions that can help mitigate its impact.

Role of Neurotransmitters: Dopamine and Serotonin

Have you ever wondered why social interactions can make you feel on top of the world one moment and completely down the next? This dramatic shift in mood often involves neurotransmitters like **dopamine and serotonin,** which play crucial roles in regulating your emotions.

Dopamine, the pleasure and reward neurotransmitter, influences your mood by regulating feelings of pleasure and reward. Imagine the thrill you feel when you receive a compliment or achieve a goal. That's dopamine at work, increasing in response to positive social interactions and reinforcing those happy feelings. When you're socially accepted or validated, your dopamine levels rise, making you feel euphoric and motivated. This boost in dopamine encourages you to seek out more positive social experiences.

However, what happens when you face rejection? Your dopamine levels can take a hit, leading to a decrease in those pleasurable feelings. This drop in dopamine can make you feel sad, unmotivated, and even hopeless. It's like going from a sunny day to a sudden storm, where everything seems bleak and heavy.

Now, let's talk about another special neurotransmitter; serotonin. Its impacts your mood and social behavior and is often referred to as the body's natural **mood stabilizer**. Serotonin helps regulate anxiety, happiness, and mood stability. Have you ever noticed how your mood dips when you haven't been sleeping well or stressed? That's because various factors can affect serotonin levels, including your overall mental health and lifestyle.

When serotonin levels are balanced, you feel calm, focused, and emotionally stable. But when they drop, perhaps due to a stressful event like rejection, you might experience heightened anxiety, depression, and emotional volatility. Low serotonin levels make it harder to bounce back from setbacks, making the pain of rejection feel more intense and prolonged.

Imagine receiving disappointing news—a job rejection or a breakup. Your brain's chemical messengers spring into action. Dopamine levels decrease, stripping away the reward and pleasure feelings, while serotonin drops, leaving you more vulnerable to negative emotions. This combination can create a potent mix of sadness, anxiety, and low self-worth.

So, what can you do to manage these biochemical responses to rejection? Here are a few tips:

- *Engage in Physical Activity:* Exercise can boost dopamine and serotonin levels, helping to improve your mood and energy levels.
- *Practice Mindfulness and Meditation:* These techniques can help stabilize your mood by promoting the release of serotonin.

- **Seek Social Support:** Positive interactions with friends and loved ones can help counteract the drop in dopamine and serotonin caused by rejection.
- **Maintain a Healthy Diet:** Foods rich in omega-3 fatty acids, vitamin D, and tryptophan (like fish, nuts, and seeds) can support the production of these neurotransmitters.

Psychological Theories

Attachment Theory

Attachment theory explores how the bonds you form in early childhood shape your emotional connections throughout life. How you interacted with your caregivers as a child lays the foundation for handling relationships and responding to rejection as an adult. These early experiences create patterns, or attachment styles, that influence your sense of security and your approach to forming connections with others.

Now, let's look at the different types of attachment styles and how they impact your response to rejection:

Secure Attachment

If you have a secure attachment style, you probably find it easier to bounce back from rejection. You tend to have a healthy self-esteem and don't see rejection as a blow to your worth. Instead, you view it as a temporary setback that doesn't define you. This confidence comes from having consistent and reliable caregivers during your early years. Because you trust that your needs will be met, you're more likely to seek support, think constructively about what happened, and move on without letting it damage your self-esteem.

Anxious Attachment

If you lean toward an anxious attachment style, rejection can feel overwhelming and trigger intense fear. You might find yourself constantly needing reassurance and approval, stemming from early experiences where caregiving was inconsistent. The fear of being abandoned or unloved makes you hypersensitive to any hint of rejection. When it happens, you may start overanalyzing every detail, blaming yourself, and worrying obsessively about future rejections. This anxiety often leads to clingy or dependent behaviors as you seek continuous validation, driven by a deep fear of being left alone.

Avoidant Attachment

If you have an avoidant attachment style, your response to rejection might be to put up emotional walls and distance yourself. On the outside, you may appear indifferent, but underneath, you could be struggling with feelings of inadequacy. This response is often a defense mechanism developed from having emotionally unavailable or dismissive caregivers. You've learned to rely on yourself and suppress your emotional needs to avoid disappointment. So, when rejection hits, you might withdraw, downplay the importance of relationships, and focus on being self-sufficient. However, this independence can mask unresolved feelings of loneliness and self-doubt.

Disorganized Attachment

For those with a disorganized attachment style, handling rejection can be especially challenging. This style often stems from early experiences of trauma or abuse, where caregivers were both a source of comfort and fear. As a result, you might find yourself swinging between anxious and avoidant behaviors, unsure of how to navigate relationships. Rejection can trigger a mix of conflicting responses—one moment you seek closeness, and the next, you push others away. Trusting others and maintaining stable relationships might feel like a constant struggle, as you grapple with overwhelming emotions and uncertainty in coping with rejection.

Your early childhood experiences with caregivers have a lasting impact on how you react to rejection as an adult. If you have a secure attachment style, you're likely to handle rejection with resilience, while those with insecure attachment styles might find it more difficult to navigate these challenges.

Social Comparison Theory

We all do it—comparing ourselves to others is a natural part of life. Social comparison theory explains how you measure your own success, happiness, and worth by looking at those around you. This habit can either lift you up or drag you down, depending on how you handle it:

Upward Comparisons

Think about the last time you scrolled through social media. Did you see a friend's vacation photos or career milestone and feel a twinge of envy? That's an upward comparison at work. When you compare yourself to someone who seems more successful or happier, it's easy to start questioning your own life. "Why am I not as successful or happy as they are?" you might wonder. These thoughts can chip away at your self-esteem, making you feel like you're not measuring up and amplifying feelings of rejection.

Downward Comparisons

On the other hand, you might find yourself feeling a bit better when you compare yourself to someone who's struggling. Maybe you think, "Well, at least I'm doing better than that person." This is a downward comparison, and while it might give you a quick confidence boost, it's not a long-term solution. Relying on these comparisons to feel good about yourself can be a way of avoiding deeper insecurities that need addressing.

However, the pervasive impact of social media has taken these comparisons to a whole new level. Platforms like Instagram, Facebook, and LinkedIn are filled with snapshots of seemingly perfect lives—curated to show the best moments and achievements. It's easy to fall into the trap of thinking everyone else has it all figured out, leaving you feeling inadequate and more sensitive to rejection. Have you ever caught yourself questioning your own choices and accomplishments after seeing someone else's "perfect" post? The constant stream of idealized lives can create a lingering sense of dissatisfaction, making you more vulnerable to social pain.

Social media doesn't just amplify these comparisons—it makes them unavoidable. With endless profiles to scroll through, it's hard not to feel like you're falling behind. This constant comparison can make rejection feel even more personal, as if others are succeeding in areas where you feel you've failed.

Additional Theories: Self-Determination & Ego Depletion

Self-Determination Theory (SDT) is a framework for understanding human motivation and behavior. It emphasizes the importance of three basic psychological needs: autonomy, competence, and relatedness. Let's explore them in detailed:

Autonomy: The need to feel in control of your actions and decisions is crucial for your psychological well-being. When you experience rejection, this sense of autonomy is often threatened. You might feel powerless and out of control, as someone else made the decision to reject you, undermining your sense of self-direction.

Competence: The need to feel effective, capable, and successful in your activities is another fundamental aspect of SDT. Rejection can lead to self-doubt and questioning your abilities, making you feel less competent. For example, being turned down for a job can make you doubt your professional skills, while a romantic rejection might make you question your attractiveness or worth as a partner.

Relatedness: The need to feel connected to others and to have meaningful relationships is essential for emotional health. Rejection directly impacts this need by creating a sense of isolation and disconnection. Whether it's social exclusion, the end of a friendship, or a breakup, rejection can make you feel as though you don't belong or are not valued by others.

When these three needs are undermined by rejection, you experience significant emotional distress. Addressing these needs through supportive relationships, self-improvement, and gaining control over your life can help mitigate the impact of rejection.

Ego Depletion, on the other hand, refers to the idea that self-control and willpower are finite resources that can be exhausted. Rejection can deplete these resources, making it harder to manage emotions and rationalize decisions. When your ego is depleted, you might react impulsively to rejection, experience heightened emotional responses, and struggle to maintain self-control. This can lead to a vicious cycle where the inability to cope effectively with rejection leads to further emotional distress and poor decision-making.

Always remember that, your self-esteem and self-worth are crucial in moderating the impact of rejection. Individuals with high self-esteem are more resilient and can better withstand the emotional blow of rejection. They will likely view rejection as a temporary setback rather than a reflection of their worth. Conversely, those with low self-esteem may internalize rejection, believing it confirms their perceived inadequacies. This internalization can make it more challenging to recover from rejection and can lead to long-term emotional distress.

End of Chapter Reflection

In this chapter, you've explored why rejection hurts so deeply through its evolutionary origins, how your brain processes it, and key psychological theories. Gaining insight into these elements helps you understand why your emotions are so intense which will help you develop effective coping strategies. Have you ever wondered why a simple "no" can sting so much? Now, you know it's not just in your head—your brain and evolutionary history play a big role. This knowledge empowers you to take the next steps towards healing and resilience. To solidify what you have learned so far, here is an action game plan for you:

- **Acknowledge Your Pain:** Recognize that your emotional response to rejection is valid and rooted in deep-seated biological and psychological processes.
- **Practice Self-Compassion:** Be kind to yourself and understand that everyone experiences rejection. It is a part of the human experience.
- **Seek Social Support:** Reach out to friends, family, or support groups to share your feelings and gain perspective.
- **Engage in Positive Activities:** Find activities that bring you joy and help distract from the pain of rejection.

- **Focus on Self-Improvement:** Use the experience of rejection as an opportunity for personal growth and development.
- **Limit Social Media Use:** Reduce exposure to social media to avoid constant comparisons that can exacerbate feelings of inadequacy.
- **Explore Professional Help:** If you find it challenging to cope with rejection on your own, consider talking to a therapist or counselor.

Journaling Prompts

- Describe a recent experience of rejection and how it made you feel.
- Reflect on how your early childhood experiences might influence your response to rejection.
- Write about ways to build resilience and improve your self-esteem in the face of rejection.
- List activities and practices that help you feel better after experiencing rejection.

The next chapter delves into the cultural and social context of rejection. It explores how societal norms, social media, and modern communication methods amplify the pain of rejection. You will discover how these factors shape the experience of rejection and learn effective ways to mitigate their impact.

Chapter 3: The Cultural and Social Context of Rejection

"Rejection doesn't mean you aren't good enough; it means the other person failed to notice what you have to offer." – Mark Amend.

C ultural norms deeply influence how you perceive and respond to rejection. Depending on whether you're part of an individualistic or collectivistic society, your experience of rejection and the way you cope with it can be quite different.

In individualistic cultures, like those in the United States and Europe, personal achievement and independence are held in high regard. You're encouraged to strive for success on your own, and with this drive comes the weight of personal responsibility for your victories and failures. But what happens when that success doesn't come? When rejection happens in such a context, it can feel intensely personal. The cultural narrative tells you that success is within your control, so when things don't go as planned, isn't it natural to question your own worth? This pressure can make any setback feel like a significant failure, leaving you feeling isolated and overwhelmed.

In these societies, rejection is often seen as a sign of personal inadequacy. Whether you're dealing with a failed job application, a missed promotion, or a romantic breakup, the rejection tends to be internalized. You might wonder, "What did I do wrong?" or "Why wasn't I good enough?" The sense of shame can be overwhelming. The idea that you should "pull yourself up by your bootstraps" can make it difficult to reach out for support, further deepening your feelings of isolation. Think about the American Dream, which promises success through hard work. When rejection strikes, does it feel like you're falling short of that ideal? Or consider the United Kingdom, where the cultural expectation to maintain a "stiff upper lip" can make it hard to openly express your feelings of rejection, leading to a sense of emotional restraint and internalized failure.

Germany's focus on precision and efficiency can make professional rejections particularly painful, turning what might be a simple setback into something that feels like a personal catastrophe. The cultural value placed on achievement and success can amplify feelings of inadequacy and discouragement, making it hard to bounce back.

On the other hand, collectivistic cultures, such as those in Japan and China, prioritize group harmony and interdependence. In these societies, the well-being of the group is more important than individual success. When you face rejection in this context, it's not just about you; it's something that affects your entire group or community. But isn't it easier to bear when you know you're not alone? The emphasis on working together and supporting one another can soften the blow of rejection, as the focus is on maintaining social cohesion rather than on individual shortcomings.

In collectivistic cultures, rejection is often viewed as a reflection on the group or community rather than just the individual. This interconnectedness means that rejection is seen as a setback for your family or community, not just for you alone. This perspective fosters a collective approach to coping, where the community comes together to offer support. For example, in Japan, the concept of "face" and the importance of maintaining social harmony means that rejection is managed in a way that minimizes embarrassment for everyone involved. In China, where familial expectations and social status are deeply intertwined, rejection becomes a family concern, with collective support playing a key role in helping you navigate the situation. In South Korea, where there's a strong cultural emphasis on education and professional success, academic or job rejections can feel like a familial failure, prompting communal support to help you recover.

But have you ever wondered how much of your reaction to rejection is shaped by the stories you've heard and the media you've consumed? Cultural narratives play a powerful role in how you deal with rejection. The stories you hear, the media you consume, and the myths you grow up with all contribute to your expectations and reactions. These narratives dictate what's considered acceptable behavior in the face of rejection. Think about the fairy tales where heroes overcome countless rejections before achieving their goals—these stories inspire resilience and perseverance. On the other hand, media portrayals often show rejection as a catalyst for personal growth, encouraging you to view setbacks as opportunities to learn and grow.

Cultural heroes who triumph over rejection show you that it's possible to overcome obstacles, while villains who let rejection define them serve as warnings of what can happen if you give in to feelings of inadequacy. These characters and stories significantly shape societal attitudes, influencing how you see yourself and how resilient you feel in the face of rejection. Positive narratives can lift your self-esteem and motivate you to keep going, while negative ones might reinforce feelings of failure and self-doubt.

As you navigate your own experiences with rejection, it's crucial to ask yourself: How much of your reaction is truly your own, and how much is shaped by the cultural and social influences around you? By recognizing these factors, you can take proactive steps to better manage your responses, turning rejection from a stumbling block into a stepping stone.

Social Media's Impact on Rejection and Self-Worth

Social media has a profound influence on how you perceive rejection and self-worth. The curated nature of these platforms often amplifies feelings of inadequacy through constant comparison and the portrayal of idealized lives.

Think about the **highlight reels** you see on social media. These aren't just random moments; they're carefully selected snapshots of people's best days—the vacations, celebrations, and successes. When you scroll through these images and posts, it's easy to start comparing your everyday life to the seemingly perfect ones portrayed online. Have you ever wondered why your life looks less exciting or polished? That's the power of **selective sharing** at work, creating a distorted view of reality that can make your own life feel lacking. The pressure to live up to these idealized portrayals can lead to constant self-evaluation and a creeping sense of dissatisfaction.

Then there's the impact of **likes, comments, and followers**—those little numbers that can seem so significant. A surge in likes can make you feel validated, like you're being seen and appreciated. But when the engagement doesn't meet your expectations, it can leave you feeling overlooked, maybe even rejected. It's easy to fall into the trap of equating these social media metrics with your self-worth. Have you noticed how your mood can shift based on the number of likes or comments a post receives? This dependency on external validation can undermine your intrinsic self-esteem, leaving you vulnerable to the whims of social media interaction.

Another challenge social media brings is **FOMO (Fear of Missing Out)**. You might see friends or acquaintances posting about parties, trips, or events that you weren't part of. This constant exposure can create a nagging feeling that you're missing out on something better, that others are living more fulfilling lives. Does it ever make you feel like you're being left behind? This fear can drive compulsive checking of social media, intensifying anxiety and creating a never-ending cycle of comparison and dissatisfaction.

And let's not forget the phenomenon of **cancel culture** and **online shaming**. Originally rooted in holding powerful figures accountable, cancel culture has now expanded to impact anyone— from celebrities to everyday individuals. A single post or comment can go viral, subjecting someone to intense scrutiny and criticism from people worldwide. Have you ever thought about how it feels to be on the receiving end of such widespread condemnation? Being publicly shamed online can lead to severe psychological distress, including anxiety, depression, and a significant loss of self-worth. The social and professional consequences can be just as damaging, with potential job loss, strained relationships, and long-lasting effects on one's mental health.

What's especially troubling about cancel culture is how enduring its effects can be. Unlike a private conversation that might be forgotten, online content sticks around, often following the individual long after the initial incident. This can lead to a persistent feeling of being judged or ostracized, making it difficult to move forward.

So, when you're engaging with social media, it's worth considering: How much of what you see is real? And how much are you allowing these platforms to shape your sense of self-worth? By being mindful of these influences, you can navigate the digital landscape with a clearer sense of what truly matters—both online and offline.

Strategies to Manage Social Media-Induced Rejection

a) Set Time Limits

Allocate specific times for social media use to prevent it from consuming your day. Setting time limits helps create a healthier balance between online and offline activities. You can use built-in app features or external apps to monitor and control the amount of time spent on social media. By scheduling dedicated time slots for social media, you can avoid the endless scrolling that often leads to feelings of inadequacy and wasted time. This intentional usage can help you stay focused and reduce the negative emotional impact of prolonged social media exposure.

b) Curate Your Feed

Follow accounts that inspire and uplift you, and unfollow those that make you feel inadequate. The content you consume on social media significantly influences your mood and self-perception. By curating your feed, you can ensure that what you see aligns with your values and positively impacts your mental health. Follow accounts that share motivational quotes, educational content, or hobbies you enjoy. Conversely, if certain accounts make you feel envious, anxious, or inadequate, it's best to unfollow or mute them to create a more positive and supportive online environment.

c) Engage Positively

Focus on positive interactions and avoid engaging in negative or inflammatory discussions. Engaging positively means liking, commenting, and sharing content that uplifts and inspires you and others. Avoid getting involved in arguments or negative debates that can escalate emotions and lead to feelings of stress or rejection. Contributing positively to your social media communities can foster a supportive network and experience more fulfilling and rewarding online interactions.

d) Take Breaks

Regularly disconnect from social media to give yourself a mental break. Taking breaks from social media allows your mind to rest and recover from the constant influx of information and comparisons. Use this time to engage in offline activities that bring you joy and relaxation, such as reading a book, going for a walk, or spending quality time with loved ones. Regular breaks can help reset your perspective and reduce the emotional toll of social media.

e) Be Mindful

Stay aware of how social media affects your mood and self-esteem, and adjust your usage accordingly. Practicing mindfulness involves paying attention to your emotional responses while using social media. Notice how different types of content make you feel and be honest with yourself about its impact. If you find that certain interactions or content consistently make you feel bad, take steps to limit exposure to those triggers. Based on this self-awareness, adjusting your social media habits can help you maintain a healthier mental state.

Setting Boundaries and Limiting Screen Time

Creating boundaries around your screen use can make a big difference in your daily life. One effective approach is to establish **screen-free zones** in your home. Think about designating certain areas, like your bedroom or dining room, as places where screens are off-limits. These zones can become special spaces for relaxation and genuine face-to-face interactions, free from the distractions of phones and tablets. Imagine how refreshing it would be to have a sanctuary where you can fully disconnect from the digital world and connect more meaningfully with the people around you.

Another strategy is to **use technology mindfully**. It's easy to fall into the habit of mindlessly scrolling through social media out of boredom or routine, but what if you used it more intentionally? Consider setting clear intentions for your online activity—maybe you're logging on to stay informed, catch up with friends, or find some inspiration. By being more deliberate about how and why you use social media, you can reduce excessive screen time and make sure it's serving your goals and well-being, rather than just filling time.

And then there's the constant barrage of notifications. Turning off **non-essential notifications** can be a simple yet powerful way to reclaim your attention. Think about how often your phone pings or vibrates, pulling you away from whatever you're doing. Disabling those unnecessary alerts can help you stay focused on what really matters, whether it's a conversation, a task, or just enjoying a quiet moment. It's amazing how much calmer and more present you can feel when you're not constantly interrupted by your phone.

Techniques for Building Resilience against Social Media Pressures

The pressures from social media can shatter your sense of self-worth, making it hard to feel secure in who you are. But you're not powerless against these influences—there are techniques you can use to build resilience and protect your mental well-being.

Start with **mindfulness practices and digital detoxes**. Have you ever noticed how a simple deep breath can help you feel more centered? Mindfulness is all about staying grounded in the present moment, and it can be a powerful tool against the constant bombardment of social media. Try incorporating meditation or deep breathing into your daily routine. These practices can help you become more aware of how social media affects your emotions, allowing you to choose how you respond rather than just reacting. And sometimes, the best thing you can do is take a break. Imagine stepping away from all your devices for a few hours or even a whole day. Doesn't that sound refreshing? Regular digital detoxes give your mind a chance to reset and reduce the stress that comes from being constantly connected. These breaks aren't just about turning off your phone—they're about reconnecting with yourself and the world around you.

But mindfulness alone isn't enough. **Developing a strong offline support network** is another crucial step. Think about the last time you had a meaningful face-to-face conversation. How did it make you feel? Real-world connections provide a kind of support that social media can't match. Spending time with friends and family, joining a club, or getting involved in your community can remind you of the value of in-person interactions. These relationships offer emotional support, practical advice, and genuine companionship—things that are hard to find online. Have you ever felt that sense of belonging when you're surrounded by people who truly care about you? That's the power of a strong offline network. It not only helps you stay grounded but also gives you a solid foundation to lean on when social media pressures start to feel overwhelming.

Building resilience against social media pressures doesn't happen overnight, but every small step you take makes a difference. Whether it's setting aside time for mindfulness, unplugging from your devices, or strengthening your real-world connections, you're taking control of your well-being. And in a world where social media often dictates how we feel about ourselves, isn't that control worth having?

End of Chapter Reflection

The cultural and social contexts you live in significantly shape your understanding and experience of rejection. These norms and influences are often so deeply ingrained that they can subtly impact your feelings and reactions without you even realizing it. Take a moment to consider the insights you've gained—how do these cultural and social forces affect you personally? Reflect on the strategies we've discussed and think about how you can apply them to navigate rejection more effectively. Are there specific cultural or social pressures in your life that you need to address?

To help you take concrete steps forward, here's an action plan to consider:

- First, limit your social media exposure. By setting specific times for when you'll engage online and taking regular breaks, you can give yourself the space to disconnect and recharge. Next, focus on cultivating positive online interactions. Engage with content and communities that inspire and uplift you, steering clear of negative or toxic discussions that can drag you down.

- It's equally important to cultivate and maintain your offline relationships. Strong, supportive connections with friends and family can serve as a protective shield against the pressures you might face online. Incorporating mindfulness practices into your daily routine can help you stay grounded and reduce the stress of navigating digital and real-world interactions. Setting clear personal boundaries for your social media use is another crucial step in safeguarding your mental well-being.

- Lastly, don't underestimate the power of seeking out success stories. Look for examples of individuals who have triumphed over rejection in ways that resonate with you. These stories can serve as a source of inspiration and a reminder that resilience is not just a concept, but a tangible reality, even in the face of setbacks.

In the next chapter, we will discuss the emotional consequences of rejection. You will learn about the common emotional responses to rejection and how they affect your mental health. Stay tuned to uncover strategies for managing the emotional fallout of rejection and finding ways to heal and grow. Remember, every step you take toward understanding and coping with rejection brings you closer to becoming a stronger, more resilient version of yourself.

PART 2

The Impact of Rejection

Chapter 4: Emotional Consequences

"Though no one can go back and make a brand new start, anyone can start from now and make a brand new ending." – Carl Bard.

R ejection can unleash several emotions that can be difficult to manage and understand. The aftermath is often marked by **grief, anger, and confusion,** each contributing to a challenging emotional journey that requires careful navigation.

Grief and the Sense of Loss

Grief is a natural response to rejection, as it involves mourning lost opportunities, relationships, and dreams. When you face rejection, you are not just dealing with the immediate pain but also the loss of what could have been. This sense of loss can be profound and multifaceted, and can lead to:

> **Lost Opportunities:** Rejection often signifies the end of a potential path or opportunity. Whether it's a job you didn't get, a relationship that ended, or a project that wasn't approved, the grief comes from the potential you saw in that opportunity. You might wonder about the possibilities and achievements that now seem out of reach.

- **Lost Relationships:** The end of a relationship, whether romantic or platonic, can lead to intense feelings of grief. This is not only about the loss of the person but also your shared experiences, mutual support, and emotional connection. The absence of these elements can create a void that is hard to fill.

- **Lost Dreams:** Dreams and aspirations often fuel our motivations and actions. When rejection shatters these dreams, it can feel like a part of your identity and future has been taken away. This can lead to a period of mourning for the future you had envisioned.

Anger: Frustration and Blame in Rejection

Anger is a common response to rejection, arising from the frustration and sense of injustice it brings. This anger can be directed both **"inward and outward".** When you direct anger inward, it often manifests as self-blame and self-criticism. You might find yourself replaying events and berating yourself for perceived mistakes. This internalized anger can be damaging, leading to a decline in self-esteem and self-worth. Outward anger, on the other hand, is directed towards others or the situation. You might blame the person who rejected you, the circumstances, or even fate. This anger can sometimes be a protective mechanism, shielding you from the vulnerability of feeling hurt and rejected.

Confusion and Self-Doubt after Rejection

Rejection often leaves you feeling lost and unsure, stirring up a whirlwind of confusion and self-doubt that can be hard to shake off. It's not uncommon to start questioning your self-worth, wondering if you're truly good enough or if there's something fundamentally wrong with you. These thoughts can creep in, eroding your confidence and making you doubt your value and abilities. It's as if every setback whispers, "Maybe I'm not cut out for this," and that self-doubt can feel paralyzing, affecting how you see yourself and your place in the world.

You might also find yourself revisiting the decisions that led to the rejection. Whether it's about a career move, a relationship choice, or a personal decision, it's easy to start second-guessing your judgment. You may ask yourself, "Did I make the right choice?" or "Should I have done something differently?" This kind of self-questioning can leave you feeling even more uncertain, as if every step you took was somehow flawed.

And then there's the fear of what comes next. The uncertainty brought on by rejection can cast a shadow over your future possibilities. You might hesitate to take new risks or pursue opportunities, worried that you'll just face rejection all over again. It's as if the sting of rejection lingers, making you wary of stepping forward, even when you know there's more you want to achieve.

But remember, these feelings of confusion and self-doubt, while painful, are also part of the process of healing and growth. As challenging as it is, each experience of rejection offers a chance to reflect, learn, and eventually, regain your confidence to move forward again.

Stages of Grief in Rejection

The stages of grief in rejection can be a complex emotional journey, and understanding each stage can help you navigate this process more effectively. Let's walk through these stages together, recognizing how each one might show up in your life and how you can work through them:

> **Denial** is often the first stage you encounter after facing rejection. It's that initial shock where your mind refuses to accept what has happened. In a romantic context, you might convince yourself that the breakup isn't real, clinging to the hope that your partner will come back. You might find yourself repeatedly reaching out, holding onto mementos, or imagining scenarios where things magically resolve. Similarly, in a professional setting, denial might look like believing the job rejection was a mistake. You

could be checking your email obsessively, replaying the interview in your head, or continuing to prepare as if you'll still get that call. When it comes to social rejection, denial can manifest as refusing to acknowledge that a friend has distanced themselves. You might continue inviting them to events or trying to maintain the same level of interaction, even when it's clear that the relationship has changed. Denial is your mind's way of protecting you from the pain, but staying in this stage can prevent you from moving forward.

As denial fades, **anger** often takes its place. This is when feelings of injustice and resentment surface. You might find yourself blaming others for the rejection, whether it's your ex-partner for not understanding you, the employer for not recognizing your talents, or a friend for drifting away. Anger can lead to irritability and outbursts, as you try to make sense of why this is happening to you. It's normal to feel angry, but it's important to channel this emotion in a way that doesn't harm yourself or others. Acknowledging your anger can be a step towards processing your feelings and eventually finding peace.

Then comes **bargaining**—that stage where you start thinking, "If only I had done something differently." It's a natural response to want to reverse or mitigate the rejection by trying to figure out what you could change.

Maybe you think, "If I just change this about myself, they'll come back," or "If I try harder, I can fix this." Bargaining is your attempt to regain control over a situation that feels out of your hands. It's a desperate plea to make things right but can also trap you in a cycle of self-blame and regret. Recognizing that some things are beyond your control can help you move past this stage.

As reality sets in, **depression** can follow, bringing with it a deep sense of sadness and withdrawal. The weight of rejection becomes more tangible, making it hard to find joy or motivation in daily life. You might feel persistently sad, struggling to shake off the gloom that seems to hang over you. Activities that once brought you happiness might now seem meaningless, leading to further isolation. This stage can also bring physical symptoms like fatigue, changes in appetite, and disrupted sleep. You may feel constantly tired, lacking the energy to engage in even the simplest tasks. Alongside this, feelings of worthlessness might creep in, convincing you that you're not good enough. This is a difficult stage but also a crucial part of the healing process. Acknowledging these feelings without judgment allows you to start addressing them.

Finally, there's **acceptance**—the stage where you begin accepting the rejection and looking forward again. Acceptance doesn't mean you're suddenly okay with what happened, but rather that you've made peace with it. You start to see rejection as a part of life that doesn't define your worth. This is where you can begin to heal, finding closure and moving forward with a renewed sense of purpose. It's about understanding that while rejection hurts, it doesn't have to hold you back.

Moving through these stages is not always linear, and you might find yourself revisiting some stages before reaching acceptance. What's important is to be kind to yourself during this time. Take care of your emotional well-being, seek support when needed, and focus on rebuilding your confidence and sense of direction. Remember, every stage you move through brings you closer to healing and resilience.

End of Chapter Reflection

In this chapter, we have explored the emotional consequences of rejection, including the feelings of grief, anger, and confusion that often accompany it. Understanding these emotional responses and the stages of grief can help you navigate the aftermath of rejection more effectively.

7-Day Emotional Healing Challenge

Here is a 7-Day Emotional Healing Challenge to help you effectively navigate and heal from the emotional consequences of rejection. Each day, you'll focus on a specific task designed to support your emotional recovery. Remember, this journey is about progress, not perfection. Take your time, be kind to yourself, and celebrate each step forward.

Day 1: Acknowledge Your Emotions

Spend 15-30 minutes reflecting on your feelings of grief, anger, and confusion. Write them down in a journal or talk them out with a trusted friend. Recognize and validate these emotions without judgment. Ask yourself, "What am I feeling right now?" and let the answers flow naturally.

Day 2: Identify Your Stage of Grief

Reflect on the stages of grief (denial, anger, bargaining, depression, acceptance) and identify which stage you are currently in. Write a brief note in your journal about your current stage and how it affects your thoughts and behavior. Understanding that this is a normal part of the healing process can be reassuring.

Day 3: Express Your Feelings

Choose a healthy outlet to express your emotions. This could be journaling, creating art, playing music, or talking to someone you trust. Spend at least 30 minutes engaging in this activity. Reflect on how expressing your feelings impacts your mood and perspective.

Day 4: Seek Professional Help

Task: Research therapists or support groups in your area. If you feel ready, schedule an appointment with a therapist or reach out to a support group. If not, note down the resources you found for future reference. Write about your feelings towards seeking professional help and how it could benefit you.

Day 5: Practice Self-Compassion

Task: Practice self-compassion today by doing something kind for yourself. This could be taking a relaxing bath, reading a favorite book, or treating yourself to something special. Spend at least 30 minutes on this self-care activity. Reflect on how self-compassion helps you feel more at ease with your emotions.

Day 6: Focus on the Present

Task: Practice mindfulness by focusing on the present moment. Spend 10-15 minutes meditating, concentrating on your breath, or engaging in a mindful activity like walking or cooking. Write about your experience and how staying present helps you manage your emotions.

Day 7: Plan for the Future

Task: Set one realistic goal for the upcoming week to help you move forward and regain your sense of purpose. It could be as simple as starting a new hobby, reconnecting with a friend, or taking a small step toward a larger ambition. Write down your goal and the steps you need to take to achieve it.

By the end of this 7-day challenge, you'll have taken significant steps toward understanding and managing the emotional fallout of rejection. Each day's task is designed to build on the previous one, helping you develop resilience and a renewed sense of purpose. Remember, healing is a journey, and you are making meaningful progress each day.

In the next chapter, we will discuss the physical manifestations of rejection. You will learn how rejection affects your body and health, and how to recognize and manage these physical symptoms.

Chapter 5: Physical Manifestations

"Your body hears everything your mind says. Stay positive and your body will thank you." – Anonymous.

Psychosomatic Responses

Emotional stress doesn't just affect your mind—it also takes a toll on your body. This is known as a **psychosomatic response**, where emotional distress manifests as physical symptoms. You might experience headaches, stomachaches, or muscle tension, all of which are signs that your body is reacting to the stress you're under. These physical symptoms serve as a reminder that the mind and body are deeply connected.

When stress triggers the release of hormones like cortisol and adrenaline, your body prepares for action—the "fight or flight" response. While this reaction is useful in short bursts, helping you respond to immediate threats, ongoing stress keeps your body in a state of constant alert. Over time, this can lead to serious health problems. High cortisol levels can weaken your immune system, making you more susceptible to illnesses and digestive issues.

Think about the fight or flight response as your body's automatic defense mechanism, kicking in without conscious effort. But when this response doesn't switch off, the chronic stress can put significant strain on your heart and blood vessels, leading to hypertension. Your digestive system might also start to suffer, with symptoms like irritable bowel syndrome (IBS) becoming more frequent. Additionally, persistent stress is a major factor in the development of anxiety, depression, and other mental health challenges.

These physical symptoms can become a constant reminder of the emotional burden you're carrying. High blood pressure, digestive problems, and a weakened immune system are just a few of the ways your body may signal that it's under too much stress. Mentally, the continuous strain can lead to a spiral of **anxiety and depression** that feels overwhelming.

Common Physical Symptoms

Let's take a moment to delve a bit deeper into the physical symptoms that often accompany rejection and explore some practical ways to manage them:

Sleep Disturbances

Rejection can disrupt your sleep patterns, leading to conditions like insomnia, where you struggle to fall or stay asleep, or hypersomnia, where you might find yourself sleeping too much. Insomnia often arises from heightened anxiety and constant rumination about the rejection, making it difficult to relax at night. On the flip side, hypersomnia can serve as an escape, a way to avoid confronting the emotional pain by retreating into sleep.

The quality of your sleep plays a crucial role in your emotional health. Poor sleep not only worsens emotional distress but also creates a vicious cycle—lack of rest impairs your ability to think clearly, manage your emotions, and handle stress. On the other hand, practicing good sleep hygiene can boost your emotional resilience, helping you cope better with rejection and other challenges.

Changes in Appetite

Rejection can also throw your appetite out of balance, leading to either emotional eating or a loss of appetite. Emotional eating is when you turn to food for comfort rather than hunger, which can result in overeating and potential weight gain. Conversely, some people might lose their appetite entirely, leading to weight loss and even nutritional deficiencies.

These changes in eating habits can lead to nutritional imbalances that impact your overall health. Emotional eating often involves consuming foods that are high in calories but low in nutrients, potentially leading to obesity, diabetes, and heart issues. On the other hand, a loss of appetite can deprive your body of essential nutrients, weakening your immune system and leaving you feeling drained and fatigued.

Headaches

Stress-induced headaches, whether tension headaches or migraines, are another common physical symptom of rejection. Tension headaches usually bring a dull, persistent ache around your head, while migraines can cause intense, throbbing pain, often accompanied by nausea and sensitivity to light and sound.

To manage these stress-induced headaches, staying hydrated is key, as dehydration is a common trigger. Regular exercise can also help, as physical activity reduces stress and releases endorphins, which are natural pain relievers. Relaxation techniques like deep breathing, meditation, and progressive muscle relaxation can ease the tension that contributes to headaches. And, of course, maintaining healthy sleep patterns is essential for keeping these headaches at bay.

Muscle Tension

Muscle tension is another physical response to the stress of rejection, often leading to tightness, pain, and stiffness, particularly in your neck, shoulders, and back. This chronic stress can make your muscles feel like they're always on edge, adding to your overall discomfort.

Managing muscle tension involves a combination of strategies. Regular stretching exercises can help relieve tightness and improve your flexibility. Massage therapy is another effective way to reduce tension and promote relaxation. Heat therapy, such as applying a warm compress, can enhance blood flow and ease pain in tense muscles. Additionally, mindfulness practices like yoga and tai chi can help you manage stress, reducing muscle tension over time.

Overall Mortality

Long-term exposure to chronic stress, including that caused by rejection, can have a significant impact on lifespan. The cumulative effect of ongoing stress can lead to various health problems that ultimately reduce life expectancy. Studies have shown that social isolation, a common consequence of rejection, is associated with a higher risk of mortality. The lack of social support and ongoing stress can lead to health issues such as cardiovascular disease, weakened immune function, and mental health disorders, all of which can shorten lifespan.

End of Chapter Reflection

You have seen how rejection can manifest in various physical ways, such as sleep disturbances, headaches, loss of appetite and even sometimes lead to mortality. Have you noticed any of these symptoms in yourself? This insight can empower you to take proactive steps to manage and alleviate these effects. Remember, taking care of your physical health is a vital part of your emotional recovery, and you have the power to improve your well-being. To solidify your understanding and put what you have learned into practice, here is an action game plan for you:

- **Practice Good Sleep Hygiene:** Establish a regular sleep routine to improve sleep quality and overall health. This includes going to bed and waking up at the same time each day, avoiding screens before bedtime, and creating a restful sleep environment. Quality sleep can help your body recover from stress and maintain emotional balance.

- **Maintain a Balanced Diet:** Focus on nutritious foods to support physical and emotional well-being. Incorporate a variety of fruits, vegetables, whole grains, and lean proteins into your diet. Proper nutrition fuels your body and mind, helping to stabilize mood and energy levels.

- **Exercise Regularly:** Engage in physical activities to reduce stress and improve overall health. Regular exercise releases endorphins, which are natural mood lifters. Aim for at least 30 minutes of moderate exercise, such as walking, running, or cycling, most days of the week.

- **Incorporate Relaxation Techniques:** Use meditation, deep breathing, and yoga to manage stress. These techniques can help calm your mind, reduce anxiety, and promote a sense of well-being. Set aside time each day to practice relaxation methods that work best for you.

- **Stay Hydrated:** Drink plenty of water to prevent dehydration-related headaches. Staying hydrated supports overall bodily functions, including brain function, which can affect your mood and stress levels. Aim for at least eight glasses of water a day.

- **Seek Social Support:** Build and maintain supportive relationships to mitigate the effects of social stress. Connect with friends, family, or support groups to share your experiences and receive emotional support. Having a strong support network can help you feel understood and less isolated.

- **Consider Professional Help:** Consult with healthcare professionals if you experience chronic physical symptoms related to stress. This might include seeing a doctor, therapist, or counselor who can provide guidance and treatment options tailored to your needs. Professional help can be crucial in managing both physical and emotional health.

In the next chapter, we will explore rejection's psychological and long-term effects. You will learn about how rejection impacts mental health over time and the enduring consequences it can have on your well-being.

Chapter 6: Psychological and Long-term Effects

"Out of your vulnerabilities will come your strength." – Sigmund Freud.

Self-Esteem Erosion

Rejection can deeply impact your self-esteem, causing a gradual decline in self-confidence and self-respect. When faced with rejection, you might start doubting your abilities and worth, leading to a pervasive sense of inadequacy. This erosion of self-esteem can be subtle at first but may intensify over time, affecting various aspects of your life. Have you noticed how a single rejection can make you question everything about yourself? This is because rejection challenges your core beliefs about your worthiness and capabilities. Signs of low self-esteem following rejection include:

Self-Doubt

Do you constantly question your abilities and decisions? This is a common sign that your self-esteem has taken a hit. You might find yourself second-guessing every choice, no matter how small, and feeling unsure about your skills and judgments. This persistent self-doubt can undermine your confidence in both personal and professional settings, making it difficult to trust your instincts and take decisive action.

Negative Self-Image

Viewing yourself as inferior or unworthy is another red flag. After experiencing rejection, you may start to see yourself in a negative light, focusing on perceived flaws and shortcomings. This negative self-image can lead to feelings of shame and a belief that you are not good enough. It can affect your interactions with others, making you more likely to withdraw and isolate yourself.

Avoidance of Challenges

Reluctance to take on new opportunities for fear of failing again often follows rejection. When your self-esteem is low, the prospect of facing another rejection can be paralyzing. You might avoid pursuing new goals, trying new things, or stepping out of your comfort zone because the fear of failure feels overwhelming. This avoidance can limit your growth and keep you stuck in a cycle of inactivity and self-doubt.

Sensitivity to Criticism

Overreacting to feedback or perceived slights can indicate deeper self-esteem issues. If you find yourself taking constructive criticism personally or feeling disproportionately upset by minor comments, it may be a sign that rejection has made you more sensitive to perceived negative judgments. This heightened sensitivity can strain relationships and make accepting and learning from feedback challenging.

Negative Self-Talk and Self-Image

Negative self-talk often accompanies rejection, where you internalize the rejection and develop a negative self-image. This internal dialogue can be harsh and self-critical, reinforcing feelings of unworthiness and failure. Combatting negative self-talk is crucial for rebuilding self-esteem and fostering a healthier self-perception. Do you catch yourself thinking, "I'm not good enough" or "I always mess things up"? These thoughts can be powerful but are often based on emotions rather than facts. To effectively combat negative self-talk, follow the tips below:

Mindfulness

Practicing mindfulness helps you become aware of negative thoughts without judgment. Are you mindful of your inner dialogue? You can identify negative self-talk patterns by staying present and observing your thoughts as they arise. Mindfulness practices, such as meditation or deep breathing exercises, can help you detach from these thoughts and reduce their impact on your self-esteem.

Positive Affirmations

Replace negative self-talk with positive affirmations about your worth and abilities. Affirmations are powerful statements that can help rewire your brain to think more positively. For example, instead of thinking, "I always fail," try telling yourself, "I am capable and resilient." Regularly repeating positive affirmations can help build a more positive self-image and reinforce your strengths.

Cognitive Behavioral Techniques

Challenge and reframe negative thoughts with evidence-based reasoning. Cognitive Behavioral Therapy (CBT) techniques involve identifying distorted thinking patterns and replacing them with more realistic and balanced thoughts. Ask yourself questions like, "What evidence do I have that supports this thought?" and "Is there an alternative explanation?" This method helps you break down negative beliefs and replace them with more constructive perspectives.

Self-Compassion

Treat yourself with the same kindness and understanding that you would offer a friend. Self-compassion involves recognizing that everyone makes mistakes and experiences setbacks. Instead of criticizing yourself harshly, practice self-forgiveness and offer yourself words of encouragement. For example, if you make a mistake, remind yourself, "It's okay to make mistakes. I am learning and growing." This approach fosters a kinder and more supportive internal dialogue.

Potential Mental Health Issues: Anxiety and PTSD

Anxiety

Rejection can lead to persistent anxiety, characterized by excessive worry and a deep-seated fear of facing future rejection. This anxiety can be so overwhelming that it starts to impact your daily life and interactions. Have you ever found yourself so worried about being rejected again that you start avoiding certain situations altogether? Maybe you skip social gatherings or shy away from opportunities because the fear of rejection is too strong. But here's the tricky part—avoiding these situations only feeds the anxiety, making it harder to break free from its grip.

When dealing with rejection-induced anxiety, you might notice certain symptoms creeping into your life. It could be a constant worry about facing rejection again, which lingers in the back of your mind, influencing your decisions and actions. You might start avoiding social situations, not because you don't want to participate, but because the fear of judgment feels too overwhelming. And then there are the physical symptoms—the racing heart, the sweating, the trembling—that show up whenever you're faced with the possibility of rejection.

But how do you cope with this kind of anxiety? One effective strategy is to practice **breathing exercises**. Have you ever tried taking deep, slow breaths when you're feeling anxious? It's a simple technique, but it can work wonders in calming your nervous system and bringing you back to the present moment. Another approach is **exposure therapy**, where you gradually face the situations you fear. By slowly building up your tolerance, you can start to reduce the anxiety that these situations trigger.

Mindfulness meditation is another powerful tool. By focusing on the present moment, you can learn to let go of worries about the future and the potential for rejection. It's about grounding yourself in the here and now, rather than letting your mind spiral into what-ifs. And if the anxiety feels too overwhelming to manage on your own, seeking **professional help** can make a significant difference. Cognitive-behavioral therapy (CBT) is specifically designed to help you reframe your thoughts and develop healthier coping mechanisms.

Each of these strategies offers a path toward managing the anxiety of rejection. It's about finding what works for you and gradually building resilience, so that rejection doesn't hold you back from living your life to the fullest

Traumatic Responses to Severe Rejection Experiences

In some cases, severe rejection can lead to post-traumatic stress disorder (PTSD), characterized by intense, distressing memories and emotional responses related to the rejection experience. Have you experienced flashbacks or nightmares about a particularly painful rejection? These intrusive symptoms can be overwhelming and significantly impact your daily life.

PTSD symptoms include **intrusive thoughts, nightmares, flashbacks,** and **severe anxiety** related to the traumatic event. These symptoms can make it difficult to function and can disrupt your emotional well-being.

Trauma-focused therapy is a specialized approach aimed at processing and healing from trauma. This type of therapy helps you work through the painful memories associated with rejection, allowing you to process and release the trauma.

EMDR (Eye Movement Desensitization and Reprocessing) is another effective technique designed to alleviate the distress connected to traumatic memories. This therapy uses guided eye movements to help you reprocess these experiences, reducing their emotional impact.

Additionally, medication may be prescribed to manage symptoms of PTSD as part of a comprehensive treatment plan. Medications can offer relief from severe anxiety and emotional distress, helping you regain stability and improve your quality of life.

Long-term Effects on Trust and Relationship-Building

Trust Issues

Rejection can severely impact your ability to trust others, making it challenging to form and maintain relationships. This difficulty often stems from the fear of being hurt again and the lingering effects of past betrayals. Do you find it hard to open up to new people or believe they have good intentions? This hesitation is a natural response to the pain you've experienced but can also create barriers to forming meaningful connections.

Rebuilding trust after rejection is a gradual process that often begins with **open communication**. Encouraging honest and transparent conversations in your relationships can help create a foundation of trust. Have you tried expressing your feelings openly? Sharing your thoughts and emotions with others, even when it feels uncomfortable, can lead to a deeper understanding and connection.

Another important aspect is **setting boundaries**. Establishing and respecting personal boundaries within your relationships can create a sense of safety and predictability, which is crucial for rebuilding trust. When both parties understand and honor each other's limits, it helps prevent misunderstandings and reduces the fear of being hurt.

Rebuilding trust also involves **gradual exposure** to vulnerability. It's does not mean to dive headfirst into deep trust; but rather taking small, deliberate steps towards being open again. Each step, no matter how small, can help you slowly regain your confidence in others.

If trust issues feel too overwhelming to tackle on your own, **therapy** can be a valuable resource. Working with a therapist can help you address deep-seated trust issues and develop healthier relationship patterns. Therapy provides a safe space to explore your fears, learn new coping strategies, and gradually rebuild your ability to trust.

Rebuilding trust takes time, but with patience and the right strategies, you can work towards healthier and more fulfilling relationships.

Fear of Intimacy

The fear of intimacy often leads you to keep relationships at arm's length, as a way to protect yourself from potential rejection. While this might feel like a safe strategy, it can also bring about loneliness and hold you back from personal growth. Are you finding yourself keeping people at a distance because the idea of getting hurt again feels too overwhelming? This fear, although understandable, can become a barrier that stops you from experiencing deep, meaningful connections.

To move past this fear, start with **self-reflection**. Think about where these feelings stem from. Are there specific relationships or moments in your past that have shaped how you approach intimacy now? Taking some time to reflect on these experiences, whether through journaling or discussing them with someone you trust, can help you uncover what's really going on beneath the surface. This understanding is the first step toward changing how you approach relationships.

Boosting self-esteem is also key to opening yourself up to love and connection. When you feel confident and value your own worth, it becomes easier to believe that you deserve meaningful relationships. Focus on activities that enhance your sense of self— setting personal goals, practicing self-care, or simply recognizing your strengths and achievements. With a stronger sense of self-worth, the idea of letting others in becomes less daunting.

You don't need to rush into deep emotional territory all at once. Start by **taking small steps** towards vulnerability. Begin by sharing something personal with a trusted friend or loved one, and as you feel more comfortable, gradually open up more. Each small step helps build trust and eases the fear of being hurt. Celebrate your progress, no matter how small, and acknowledge the courage it takes to open up.

If this fear feels too big to tackle alone, **seeking support** can be incredibly helpful. Talk to a trusted friend or consider working with a therapist who provides guidance. Having someone who listens and validates your feelings can provide the comfort and encouragement you need. A therapist, in particular, can help you work through these fears and develop healthier relationship patterns, making it easier to build deeper connections.

As you begin to address the fear of intimacy, you open yourself to the possibility of stronger, more rewarding relationships. Every small step forward brings you closer to the connections you deserve, helping you create a richer, more connected life.

Social Withdrawal

Rejection can sometimes push you to withdraw from social activities, leading you to isolate yourself in an attempt to avoid further hurt. While this might feel like self-protection, it often deepens feelings of loneliness and can worsen mental health struggles. Have you noticed yourself pulling away from the social activities and people you once enjoyed?

To counteract this, consider re-engaging with the world around you. **Joining groups or clubs** that align with your interests can be a great way to meet new people and form connections. **Volunteering** is another way to immerse yourself in a community, offering both a sense of purpose and the chance to build meaningful relationships. It's also important to **maintain existing relationships** by putting effort into nurturing the friendships and family connections you already have. Remember, relationships require time and effort, so you must set **realistic expectations** as you build and maintain them.

End of Chapter Reflection

To be honest, facing rejection is one of the hardest things we go through. It's that deep, lingering ache that makes you question your worth and wonder if you'll ever feel whole again. You've seen how rejection can seep into every corner of your life—eroding your self-esteem, shaking your mental health, and making it difficult to trust and connect with others. It's okay to admit that it hurts, more than you might want to let on. But in acknowledging this pain, you open the door to healing.

You're not alone in this. Recognizing the toll that rejection takes is the first step toward reclaiming your life. It's about understanding that your feelings are valid, that the impact on your heart is real, and that you have the strength to rise above it. Building resilience isn't about ignoring the hurt; it's about facing it, embracing it, and then gently guiding yourself toward the light on the other side. You deserve healthier, more fulfilling connections—with others and yourself.

Let's take a gentle, yet deliberate, approach to healing with this 7-Day Action Plan:

> On **Day 1**, take a moment to reflect and journal. Write down a recent rejection that stung deeply. Pour out your heart onto the page—how did it affect your self-esteem? What emotions did it stir up? Be honest about the negative self-talk that crept in, and then, as you read your words, think about how you can reframe those thoughts with kindness.

> **Day 2** is about practicing self-compassion. Treat yourself with the tenderness you would offer a dear friend. Engage in activities that bring you joy, whether it's a hobby you love, a workout that lifts your spirits, or simply a few moments of quiet relaxation. Today, it's all about feeling good in your own skin.

> On **Day 3**, reach out. Call a friend, spend time with family—nurture those relationships that remind you of who you are at your core. Let the conversations be

meaningful, let them heal some of the wounds that rejection has left behind.

By **Day 4**, you'll start to challenge those negative thoughts that have been weighing you down. When a dark thought surfaces, don't just accept it—challenge it. Replace it with affirmations that remind you of your worth, your strength, your undeniable value.

Day 5 is for setting boundaries. Reflect on your relationships—where do you feel overextended or unprotected? Identify those areas and think about how you can establish or reinforce your boundaries. It's about creating a space where you feel safe and respected.

On **Day 6**, get moving. Choose a physical activity that you enjoy, something that makes you feel alive. Whether it's a brisk walk, a dance class, or a solo jog, let the movement help you shake off some of the emotional weight you've been carrying.

Finally, on **Day 7**, look to the future. Set small, achievable goals that will help you rebuild your confidence. What do you want to accomplish in the weeks ahead? Focus on personal growth—on taking those first steps toward the dreams and aspirations that rejection tried to steal from you.

This week is about reclaiming your narrative. You've been knocked down, but you're not out. Each day is a step toward healing, toward rediscovering the parts of you that rejection can never touch. You are stronger than you know, and you deserve to walk this path with your head held high, knowing that you are worthy of love, respect, and a life that fulfills you. The journey isn't easy, but it's yours—and that makes it beautiful.

The upcoming chapter will explore acknowledging and accepting your pain. You'll discover practical steps to process rejection, helping you manage the initial shock and pain effectively. This will equip you with techniques to move forward with greater resilience and clarity.

PART 3

Preparing for Healing

Chapter 7: Acknowledging and Accepting Your Pain

"Healing takes time, and asking for help is a courageous step." – Mariska Hargitay.

We've touched on this before, but now, let's look deeper into the importance of acknowledging and accepting your pain. It's easy to brush off your emotions, telling yourself that you should just "get over it" or that your feelings don't really matter. But deep down, you know that this isn't true. Your feelings are real, and they deserve to be recognized. Have you ever noticed how a weight seems to lift when you finally admit that you're hurt? That's because acknowledging your pain is the first step toward true healing. It's not about dwelling on your hurt, but about giving yourself permission to feel what you feel and to understand the root of that pain.

Validating Feelings

Recognizing your emotions is not just a step—it's an integral part of your healing journey. It's common to try and push away uncomfortable feelings, convincing yourself that you should just move on. But the truth is, those feelings don't just disappear because you ignore them. They linger, affecting your mental and emotional well-being in ways you might not even realize. When you allow yourself to acknowledge what you're going through, you're giving yourself the space to heal. Think back to a time when you felt a sense of relief after admitting that something hurt you. That simple act of validation can be incredibly powerful, connecting you more deeply with your inner self and helping you understand where your pain is coming from.

Self-reflection becomes a powerful tool in this process. It goes beyond just thinking about your feelings—it's a way to process your emotions and gain clarity on what's really going on inside. You need to incorporate journaling here. Setting aside a few minutes each day to write about what's on your mind can make a world of difference. You might start with simple questions like, "What am I feeling right now?" or "What triggered these emotions?" As you write, patterns in your thoughts and feelings may begin to emerge, offering insights that make understanding and managing them easier. There's something about putting pen to paper that can make your thoughts feel more tangible, more manageable, and somehow less overwhelming.

Sometimes, thinking and writing about your emotions isn't enough—you need to actively work through them. **Guided exercises** can be incredibly helpful here. Imagine finding a quiet space, sitting comfortably, and closing your eyes. As you take a few deep breaths, picture a warm, comforting light surrounding you, offering safety and peace. As this light envelops you, allow yourself to bring up any feelings of rejection or pain. Visualize these emotions being gently held by this light, soothing them, and helping you accept them for what they are—part of your journey, but not the entirety of who you are.

Another approach is to connect with how your emotions manifest physically. Have you ever tried a **body scan?** It's a simple yet powerful exercise. Lie down in a comfortable position, close your eyes, and slowly move your attention through your body, from the top of your head to the tips of your toes. Notice any areas where you feel tension or discomfort, and just acknowledge these sensations without trying to change them. This practice helps you understand how your emotions are physically showing up in your body, giving you a deeper connection to yourself. It's a way to honor what you're going through, recognizing that your pain is real and that it impacts you in tangible ways.

And let's talk about **self-compassion**—something we all need more of. Stand in front of a mirror, look into your own eyes, and speak to yourself with the kindness and understanding you would offer a dear friend. Say to yourself, "I am worthy of love and acceptance," or "It's okay to feel hurt; I will heal." These aren't just words—they're affirmations reminding you that you deserve the same compassion you so readily give others. Speaking kindly to yourself helps to reinforce positive self-talk and encourages a nurturing attitude toward your own healing.

Combining these exercises with regular journaling and mindfulness practices creates a comprehensive approach to processing your emotions. You're not just moving on—you're moving through your pain, with grace and strength, toward a place of greater peace and self-understanding. Each step you take in this process brings you closer to healing, helping you build a deeper connection with yourself and paving the way for a brighter, more resilient future.

Building a Support Network

To effectively build a support network, start by identifying the people in your life who can genuinely offer you the support you need. These might be family members, friends, or even colleagues who have shown empathy and understanding in the past. Think about your relationships and consider who you feel most comfortable opening up to. Sometimes, the people who can provide the most support aren't immediately obvious, so take a moment to reflect on who has been there for you during tough times—those who have offered a listening ear or a shoulder to cry on. These individuals can provide the emotional support you need to move forward.

Once you've identified these supportive individuals, it's important to reach out and nurture those relationships. Share your feelings and experiences with them, and let them know how they can support you. It might feel vulnerable at first, but reaching out is a crucial step in building a reliable support network. Ask yourself, "Who can I trust with my feelings?" and consciously connect with them. Remember, support is a two-way street; being there for others can also strengthen your own sense of connection and community. But how do you communicate your needs effectively?

Start by being clear and direct about what you're experiencing and how others can help. Have you ever tried using "I" statements to express your feelings? For example, saying, "I feel overwhelmed and could use some support," is much more effective than, "You never help me when I'm stressed." This approach helps others understand your perspective without feeling blamed or defensive. It opens the door for them to provide the support you're seeking.

It's also essential to be specific about the type of support you need. Do you need someone to listen without offering advice? Or perhaps you're looking for practical help with daily tasks? Being clear about your needs can prevent misunderstandings and ensure you get the kind of support most beneficial to you. For instance, you might say, "I need someone to talk to for a few minutes," or "Could you help me with this project I'm struggling with?" When you make specific requests, it becomes much easier for others to provide meaningful support.

As you navigate these conversations, be open to feedback and willing to adjust your expectations. Communication is a two-way process, and your friends and family might have their own perspectives on how best to support you. Encouraging an open

dialogue where both parties feel heard and respected can strengthen your relationships and create a more supportive environment. It's not just about expressing your needs but also about listening and adapting to the responses of those around you.

Have you ever considered seeking professional help as part of your support network? Therapists are trained to help you navigate complex emotions and develop strategies for healing. If you're thinking about therapy, start by exploring different types of therapy to find one that suits your needs. For example, Cognitive-Behavioral Therapy (CBT) is effective for addressing negative thought patterns, while trauma-focused therapy can help process specific rejection-related trauma. Imagine having a professional guide to help you through this journey—doesn't that sound reassuring?

Support groups can also be a valuable resource. Have you thought about joining one? These groups provide a safe space to share your experiences with others who are facing similar challenges. Being part of a support group can reduce feelings of isolation and offer comfort in knowing you're not alone. Whether you look for local or online support groups focused on rejection, self-esteem, or emotional healing, joining these communities can offer you practical advice and emotional support from people who truly understand what you're going through.

As you work on building your support network, remember that it's about creating connections that help you feel seen, heard, and valued. Whether through personal relationships or professional support, each step you take brings you closer to a stronger, more resilient version of yourself.

Self-Care Fundamentals

Maintaining physical health is a key part of self-care that directly impacts emotional well-being. Let's discuss three essential components: **a balanced diet, regular exercise, and adequate sleep.**

Eating nutritious foods gives your body the energy and nutrients it needs to function well. Focus on a diet rich in fruits, vegetables, whole grains, and lean proteins. These foods support your physical health and enhance your mental clarity and emotional stability. Think about how a colorful salad or a hearty bowl of oatmeal can boost your mood and energy levels throughout the day.

Regular exercise is another important aspect of self-care. Physical activity releases endorphins, which are natural mood lifters. Whether you enjoy a **brisk walk, a yoga session, or a workout at the gym,** find an exercise routine that you look forward to and can stick to. Aim for at least **30 minutes** of moderate exercise most days of the week. Exercise helps reduce stress, improves overall health, and boosts your confidence. Have you ever noticed how a good workout can make you feel accomplished and more positive about yourself?

Adequate sleep is vital for both physical and emotional health. Establishing a regular sleep routine ensures you get enough rest each night. Create a calming bedtime routine by turning off screens an hour before bed, practicing relaxation techniques, and keeping your sleep environment comfortable and free from distractions. Quality sleep helps your body recover from the day's stresses and prepares you to face the next day with resilience and clarity.

End of Chapter Reflection

In this chapter, you've learned to embrace your emotions, create a strong support system, and prioritize self-care. It's not always easy to face these parts of yourself, but acknowledging them is essential to healing. As you think about the insights you've gained, consider how they can become part of your daily life. Self-care isn't just about occasional moments of rest—it's about finding those practices that truly resonate with you and making them a regular part of your routine. These small, daily acts of kindness toward yourself are what will support your healing journey.

Take a moment to imagine how different your life could feel when you consistently nurture yourself. When you allow yourself the space to feel, connect, and care for your needs, you're building a foundation of resilience that will carry you through even the toughest times. This isn't just about surviving—it's about finding a way to thrive, even in the face of challenges.

Journaling Prompts

Each day, take a few minutes in the evening to check in with yourself. Reflect on the emotions you experienced throughout the day. How did you respond to them? Did you allow yourself to feel, or did you try to push them away? What self-care practices did you turn to, and how did they affect your mood and energy? Writing these reflections down can help you see the patterns in your emotions and responses, guiding you toward more intentional self-care.

Think about setting some self-care goals for yourself this week. What are three things you can do to care for yourself? Maybe it's as simple as taking a walk, spending time with a loved one, or setting aside a few minutes for quiet reflection. Write down these goals and think about how you'll incorporate them into your daily routine. How will you know when you're making progress? Sometimes, just acknowledging the effort you're putting into caring for yourself is enough to keep you going.

Also, reflect on the people in your life who offer you support. Who are the ones you can turn to when things get tough? How can you strengthen those relationships? Think about how you can communicate your needs more effectively and deepen those connections. Remember, it's okay to ask for support—true strength comes from knowing when to lean on others.

As you move forward, remember that each step you take toward embracing your emotions, caring for yourself, and building a support network is a step toward healing.

The next chapter will guide you through practical steps to overcome rejection using the SMART criteria—a powerful tool to help you set Specific, Measurable, Achievable, Relevant, and Time-bound goals. With these strategies, you'll learn how to process rejection, rebuild your self-esteem, and develop the resilience needed to face future challenges with confidence and grace.

Chapter 8: SMART Strategies and Boundaries for Overcoming Rejection

"Every rejection is incremental payment on your dues that in some way will be translated back into your work." - James Lee Burke.

To effectively navigate the aftermath of rejection, it's crucial to set **clear goals** and establish **healthy boundaries**. These two practices can help you regain control, build resilience, and confidently move forward.

SMART Goals

Let's start with the concept of **SMART goals**. Setting goals might seem daunting after experiencing rejection, but it's a powerful way to reclaim your sense of purpose. Have you ever felt lost, unsure of your next step? **SMART goals—Specific, Measurable, Achievable, Relevant, and Time-bound**—provide a structured approach to guide you through the healing process. For example, instead of vaguely deciding to "move on" after a rejection, you could set a goal like, "I will update my resume and apply to three jobs that align with my skills and passions by the end of the month." This clarity helps you focus on what you can control and makes your progress tangible, step by step.

Specific goals allow you to break down overwhelming tasks into manageable pieces. It's like building a ladder, each rung representing a small, achievable step. As you climb, you're not just moving away from rejection—you're moving toward something meaningful that reflects your true potential. How empowering would it feel to look back and see how far you've come, one small victory at a time?

Setting Healthy Boundaries

Now, let's talk about **boundaries**. Rejection can make you feel vulnerable, sometimes leading you to question your self-worth. Establishing healthy boundaries is a way to protect your emotional well-being and ensure that your relationships are based on mutual respect and understanding. Boundaries aren't about shutting people out; they're about knowing where you end and others begin. Have you ever felt drained after spending time with someone, unsure why you're so exhausted? It might be because your boundaries weren't clear, and you ended up giving more of yourself than you intended.

Setting boundaries starts with **self-awareness**. Think about what makes you feel safe and respected in your interactions with others. Is it having alone time to recharge, or perhaps feeling heard without judgment? Once you identify these needs, the next step is to communicate them clearly. It might feel uncomfortable at first, but saying something as simple as, "I need some time to myself after work to unwind," can make a huge difference in how you experience your relationships.

Boundaries are also about **prioritizing your well-being**. It's okay to say no to things that don't serve you, whether it's an extra project at work or a social event that you're not up for. Remember, **self-care isn't selfish**—it's essential. By setting boundaries, you're teaching others how to treat you, but more importantly, you're showing yourself that your needs matter.

As you integrate SMART goals and healthy boundaries into your life, you'll find that they work together to create a more balanced and empowered version of yourself. Each time you set a goal and take steps toward it or establish a boundary and stand by it, you're reinforcing your self-worth. This isn't just about overcoming rejection; it's about transforming the way you approach life— turning setbacks into stepping stones for growth.

End of Chapter Reflection

Take a moment to reflect on the strategies we've discussed. How can you start incorporating **SMART goals** and **setting boundaries** into your daily life? Think about the areas where you need to take action, and consider how these practices can help you rebuild your confidence and protect your emotional well-being.

Journaling Prompts

Reflect on a recent rejection you faced. How did you handle it, and what can you learn from the experience? Consider setting three **SMART goals** that will help you move forward. How do these goals make you feel, and what steps will you take to achieve them? Also, think about your personal boundaries—are there areas where you need to establish clearer limits in your life? How will you communicate these boundaries to others?

The next chapter will explore long-term strategies for building emotional resilience. These tools will help you turn rejection challenges into personal growth and empowerment opportunities.

PART 4

Long-term Strategies for Emotional Resilience

Chapter 9: Fortifying Your Emotional Well-being

"The greatest glory in living lies not in never falling, but in rising every time we fall." - Nelson Mandela.

Building emotional resilience is essential for navigating life's challenges. You must be reminded that every setback offers an opportunity to learn and grow. Facing difficulties with a positive outlook can transform obstacles into stepping stones for personal development. Each experience, whether positive or negative, contributes to your overall strength and resilience. Embrace these moments as they shape your journey towards a more resilient and empowered self.

Techniques for Developing a Resilient Mindset

a) Growth Mindset

To fully understand the concept of a growth mindset, it's important to differentiate between fixed and growth mindsets. A fixed mindset believes that abilities and intelligence are static traits, leading to a fear of failure and avoidance of challenges. In contrast, a growth mindset embraces challenges and views failure as an opportunity to learn and grow. Imagine seeing each obstacle as a stepping stone rather than a roadblock. This shift in perspective can make a huge difference in how you handle setbacks. Here are some practical steps to cultivate a growth mindset:

Embrace Challenges

Think of challenges as opportunities to learn and grow. When faced with a difficult task, remember that every effort you make is a step towards improvement. Stepping out of your comfort zone allows you to tackle new challenges head-on, fostering resilience and adaptability. Are you willing to embrace new experiences and push your boundaries?

Learn from Criticism

Instead of taking feedback personally, use it as a tool for growth. Criticism can offer valuable insights into areas where you can improve. Next time you receive constructive feedback, consider how it can help you refine your skills and strategies. Ask yourself, "What can I learn from this feedback, and how can I apply it to grow?"

Celebrate Effort, Not Just Success

Recognize and appreciate your hard work, regardless of the outcome. Acknowledging your persistence and dedication can boost your motivation and self-esteem. Have you taken a moment to appreciate your efforts and progress, even if the results aren't perfect?

Persist in the Face of Setbacks

Understand that setbacks are a part of the learning process. When things don't go as planned, view it as a temporary hurdle rather than a permanent failure. Reframing setbacks as opportunities to learn and grow, you can maintain your momentum and stay focused on your goals. How can you use a recent setback as a stepping stone to future success?

Focus on Learning

Prioritize acquiring new skills and knowledge over simply proving your abilities. Approach each task to learn something new. This mindset fosters continuous improvement and curiosity. What new skill or area of knowledge are you excited to explore, and how can it contribute to your personal growth?

b) Emotional Regulation

Emotional regulation is part of your journey to well-being. It involves recognizing what you are feeling and why, without judging yourself. This awareness allows you to address your emotions constructively, preventing them from overwhelming you or causing unnecessary stress. Here are a few strategies for managing and expressing emotions healthily:

Mindfulness Meditation

Sitting quietly and observing your thoughts without judgment can be incredibly grounding. Mindfulness meditation helps you stay present and aware of your emotional patterns. Dedicating a few minutes each day to this practice allows you to respond to your emotions more calmly and with greater understanding. This regular practice helps to build emotional resilience and clarity.

Deep Breathing Exercises

Deep breathing is a simple yet powerful method to calm the mind and reduce stress. Techniques such as the 4-7-8 breathing method—inhaling for four seconds, holding your breath for seven seconds, and exhaling slowly for eight seconds—can significantly alleviate anxiety and promote relaxation. Incorporating deep breathing exercises into your daily routine can enhance your ability to manage stress effectively.

Physical Activity

Regular exercise is an excellent way to release tension and improve your mood. Activities like brisk walking, running, or yoga sessions help clear your mind and uplift your spirits. Engaging in physical activity not only benefits your physical health but also has a profound positive impact on your emotional well-being, helping to reduce feelings of stress and anxiety.

Creative Outlets

Channeling your emotions through creative activities such as art, music, or writing can be incredibly therapeutic. Painting, playing an instrument, or writing about your feelings allows you to express yourself in ways that words alone might not capture. These creative outlets provide a valuable means of processing and releasing emotions, fostering a sense of relief and understanding.

Journaling

Writing about your feelings can offer clarity and insight into your emotional state. Taking time each day to jot down your thoughts and emotions helps you reflect on your experiences and better understand your emotional landscape. Journaling provides a private space to explore your feelings, leading to greater emotional awareness and personal growth.

c) Self-Compassion

Being kind to oneself is crucial for navigating difficult emotions without harsh self-judgment. Self-compassion means treating yourself with the same kindness and understanding you would offer a friend. Positive self-talk is a key technique for practicing self-compassion. Replace self-criticism with supportive and encouraging words. For instance, instead of saying, "I can't do anything right," try, "I'm doing my best, and that's enough." This shift in self-talk helps reinforce your worth and capabilities.

The Role of Gratitude and Positive Thinking in Resilience

Daily gratitude journaling can significantly boost your mental health. Start each day by writing down three things you're grateful for. This practice shifts your focus from what's missing to what's abundant in your life, fostering a more positive outlook. As you maintain this habit, you'll begin to notice the positive aspects of your life more readily.

Positive affirmations also play a vital role in building resilience. Create affirmations that align with your goals and values, such as "I am resilient and capable." Repeating these affirmations daily reinforces a positive mindset and keeps you motivated. Integrating affirmations into your routine constantly reminds you of your strengths and potential.

Exercises to Strengthen Emotional Resilience Over Time

Your daily routines play a crucial role in shaping your emotional well-being. By starting and ending your day with intention, you create a balanced and resilient mindset that can carry you through life's challenges. Here are some practical tips for both morning and evening routines:

Morning Routines

Begin your day with a few minutes of quiet meditation. This simple practice centers your mind, helping you approach the day calmly and focused. If you're new to meditation, consider using a guided meditation app or simply sitting quietly and focusing on your breath. This moment of stillness sets a peaceful tone for whatever lies ahead.

After your meditation, try incorporating positive affirmations into your morning. Affirmations like "I am capable and strong" or "I can handle whatever comes my way today" can uplift your mood and boost your confidence. Whether you write them down or say them out loud, these affirmations reinforce positive thoughts and help you start the day with optimism.

Adding some light physical activity to your morning routine can also make a big difference. Engage in gentle exercises like stretching or taking a short walk – this simple act energizes both your body and mind, making you feel more alert and ready to tackle the day's tasks. Even a few minutes of stretching can leave you feeling refreshed and invigorated.

Evening Routines

Just as your morning routine sets the tone for the day, your evening routine helps you wind down and prepare for restful sleep. Reflective journaling is a great way to end your day. Take some time to write about your experiences—what went well, what you learned, and any positive moments. This reflection allows you to process your thoughts and emotions, giving you a sense of closure and clarity. Plus, it's a wonderful way to track your progress over time.

Incorporating relaxation techniques into your evening can further enhance your ability to unwind. Deep breathing or gentle yoga can help calm your mind and relax your body, easing the transition to sleep. Even just a few deep breaths or a simple yoga pose can work wonders in preparing you for a good night's rest.

Another important aspect of your evening routine is a digital detox. Try turning off screens an hour before bed. The blue light emitted from screens can disrupt your sleep cycle, making it harder to fall asleep. Instead, consider reading a book, listening to soothing music, or engaging in another calming activity to help your mind and body prepare for sleep.

Long-term Habits

Establishing and nurturing healthy relationships is vital for emotional resilience. Surround yourself with people who support and uplift you. Engage in open and honest communication to strengthen these bonds, and make time for meaningful interactions. Building trust and mutual respect in your relationships can provide a strong foundation for emotional support.

Engaging in Regular Physical Activity

Regular physical activity is key to maintaining both physical and emotional health. Plan a weekly exercise routine that includes a mix of cardio, strength training, and flexibility exercises. Here's a simple one-week exercise plan to get you started:

Monday: 30 minutes of brisk walking or jogging to boost your cardiovascular health.

Tuesday: 20 minutes of strength training using bodyweight exercises to build muscle.

Wednesday: 30 minutes of yoga or stretching to enhance flexibility and reduce stress.

Thursday: 30 minutes of cycling or swimming for a low-impact cardio workout.

Friday: 20 minutes of high-intensity interval training (HIIT) to improve overall fitness.

Saturday: 45 minutes of hiking or a long walk to enjoy nature and stay active.

Sunday: Rest day or gentle stretching to allow your body to recover.

Maintaining a Balanced Diet

A balanced diet is essential for overall well-being. Focus on consuming whole foods such as fruits, vegetables, lean proteins, and whole grains. When shopping, choose fresh produce and avoid processed foods high in sugar and unhealthy fats. Here are some foods to avoid:

Sugary Snacks: Foods with high sugar content can lead to energy crashes and mood swings. Examples include candy bars, cookies, pastries, and sugary cereals. These foods may provide a quick burst of energy but often result in a rapid drop in blood sugar levels, leaving you tired and irritable.

Processed Foods: These often contain unhealthy additives and lack essential nutrients. Examples include food items, snacks like chips and crackers, and frozen meals. Processed foods are typically high in sodium, preservatives, and artificial flavors, which can negatively impact your health over time.

Trans Fats: Found in many fried and baked goods, they can negatively impact heart health. Examples include commercially baked cookies, cakes, pies, and certain margarines. Trans fats can increase bad cholesterol levels (LDL) while lowering good cholesterol levels (HDL), increasing the risk of heart disease.

Sugary Beverages: Drinks like soda, energy drinks, and sweetened coffees or teas are high in sugar and provide little nutritional value. Regular consumption can lead to weight gain, increased blood sugar levels, and dental problems.

Refined Grains: Foods made with white flour, such as white bread, pasta, and rice, can cause spikes in blood sugar levels and lack the fiber found in whole grains. Opt for whole grain alternatives like whole wheat bread, brown rice, and quinoa.

Pursuing Hobbies and Activities That Bring Joy

Engaging in hobbies and activities that bring you joy and fulfillment is essential for enhancing emotional resilience over the long term. Whether it's painting, gardening, playing a musical instrument, or any other passion, making time for these activities can significantly boost your mood and overall well-being. Have you noticed how much better you feel when you immerse yourself in something you truly love?

Take **painting**, for example. it's a way to express your creativity and channel your emotions into something tangible. Whether you're a beginner or a seasoned artist, painting can be incredibly therapeutic. It offers a sense of accomplishment and joy that comes from creating something unique. Have you ever felt the stress melt away as you lose yourself in your art? Experimenting with different styles and mediums can be a fun way to discover what resonates with you. Why not set aside some time each week to dive into your creative world and see where it takes you?

Then there's **gardening**—a hobby that connects you with nature and brings a deep sense of peace and fulfillment. Tending to plants, watching them grow, and nurturing life can be incredibly rewarding. Gardening isn't just about the plants; it's about the calmness and grounding that comes from working with the earth. Even if you only have space for a few potted plants, the act of caring for them can bring immense satisfaction. Have you ever experienced the joy of harvesting something you grew yourself? The process, from planting to harvest, offers a simple yet profound pleasure.

Playing a musical instrument is another wonderful way to relax and unwind. Music has the power to elevate your mood and provide an outlet for your emotions. Whether you're playing the piano, strumming a guitar, or practicing the violin, music engages both your mind and body, offering a full sensory experience that can reduce anxiety and lift your spirits. Regular practice not only helps you improve your skills but also gives you a sense of progression and achievement. Have you thought about joining a group or taking lessons to stay motivated and connect with others who share your passion for music?

Making time for hobbies like these provides a necessary break from daily stress and fosters a sense of accomplishment and joy.

By integrating these activities into your routine, you'll find that they do more than just fill your time—they enhance your emotional resilience, helping you lead a more balanced and fulfilling life.

Maintaining Healthy Relationships

a) Trust, Communication, Mutual Respect

Trust, communication, and mutual respect are the cornerstones of any healthy relationship. Building trust involves being reliable and honest with each other. Trust grows over time as you consistently show that you are dependable and have each other's best interests at heart. For instance, keeping promises and being truthful, even when it's difficult, helps establish a strong foundation of trust.

Effective communication is essential for deeper connections. When you express your thoughts and feelings openly and honestly while also being receptive to your partner's perspectives, it strengthens your bond. Techniques such as active listening, using "I" statements to express your feelings without blaming, and asking open-ended questions to encourage dialogue can greatly enhance your communication skills. This kind of communication helps understand each other's needs and resolve misunderstandings before they escalate into conflicts.

Mutual respect is vital for sustaining relationships. Key elements of respect include valuing each other's opinions, recognizing boundaries, and treating one another with kindness and consideration. Respectful relationships allow for individuality and differences without judgment. Showing appreciation for each other's contributions and acknowledging your partner's strengths can foster a positive and supportive relationship environment.

b) Setting Healthy Boundaries

Boundaries define acceptable and unacceptable behavior, protecting your emotional well-being and ensuring that both partners feel respected and valued. Think about times when you've felt overwhelmed or taken for granted—were boundaries being crossed? Knowing your limits and being clear about them prevents feelings of resentment and burnout.

Communicating and enforcing boundaries effectively requires clear and assertive communication. Use "I" statements, like "I feel overwhelmed when..." to express your needs directly yet respectfully. Explaining the reasons behind your boundaries helps your partner understand your perspective, reducing the chance of conflict. Have you tried this approach in your relationship? Listening and respecting your partner's boundaries is crucial, fostering a balanced and harmonious connection.

Balancing personal needs with relationship demands involves recognizing that both partners have individual needs and desires. It's about finding a middle ground where both can feel satisfied. Regularly checking in with each other about your boundaries and adjusting them as necessary keeps the relationship healthy and supportive. How often do you and your partner discuss your boundaries? These conversations can help ensure that both of you feel heard and valued.

c) Effective Communication Skills and Conflict Resolution Strategies

Active Listening

The art of listening with empathy and understanding is a powerful tool in maintaining healthy relationships. Active listening means fully concentrating, understanding, responding, and remembering what the other person is saying. It's about connecting with the emotions and intentions behind the words, not just hearing them. Imagine how much more connected you'd feel if your partner truly understood not just your words, but your feelings too.

To improve your active listening skills, maintain eye contact to show you are engaged, nod to indicate you are following along, and provide feedback by summarizing what you've heard. Avoid interrupting and allow the speaker to finish their thoughts. Have you ever tried summarizing your partner's words before responding? It can make them feel truly heard and valued. These practices enhance your listening abilities and make your partner feel respected and understood.

The benefits of active listening in resolving conflicts are significant. When both partners feel understood, it reduces defensiveness and opens the door for more constructive conversations. Think about a time when you felt truly listened to—how did it change the dynamic of the conversation? Active listening helps identify the root causes of conflicts and find mutually agreeable solutions, fostering a deeper connection and understanding.

Negotiation and Compromise

Finding mutually acceptable solutions is essential in any relationship. Negotiation involves discussing each other's needs and finding a solution that satisfies both parties. It's about being flexible and willing to make adjustments. Have you ever considered what a win-win solution might look like in your relationship?

Effective negotiation without compromising self-worth includes being clear about your needs, listening to your partner's perspective, and aiming for win-win solutions. Approaching negotiations with a collaborative mindset rather than a competitive one makes a huge difference. When both partners see themselves as part of the same team, reaching agreements that benefit both is easier.

Building constructive dialogue and compromise habits helps maintain harmony and understanding in the relationship. This encourages both partners to work together towards common goals, strengthening the relationship over time. Reflect on your recent disagreements—how often did you look for common ground? Practicing these skills can transform conflicts into opportunities for growth and cooperation.

d) Maintaining Independence and Self-Worth in Relationships

Keeping your personal interests and passions alive is essential for a healthy relationship. Having activities and hobbies that you enjoy individually brings a sense of fulfillment and happiness. Imagine the joy of sharing new experiences and insights with your partner after spending time on something you love. This boosts your personal growth and infuses fresh energy into your relationship.

Scheduling regular alone time is key. Think about setting aside specific times each week for solo activities. Pursuing individual interests and encouraging your partner to do the same helps maintain a balance where both of you can grow independently while nurturing your connection. Have you ever noticed how spending time apart can make your moments together even more special?

You must ensure that your self-worth isn't solely dependent on the relationship. Recognize and appreciate your own value. Building a strong sense of self outside the relationship is crucial. Achieve this through personal achievements, self-reflection, and maintaining healthy self-esteem. When you value yourself, you bring a sense of completeness and stability to the relationship. Reflect on your recent personal successes—how do they make you feel? Valuing yourself contributes positively to the relationship, enhancing both your well-being and the bond you share with your partner.

Preventing Future Heartbreak

Identifying red flags and deal breakers early in a relationship can prevent future heartbreak. It involves being aware of behaviors and patterns that indicate potential issues and knowing when to enforce personal boundaries. Recognizing these early signs lets you make informed decisions about whether to continue or end the relationship, ensuring your emotional well-being is protected. Here are some of the most common red flags in relationship:

Lack of Communication: If your partner consistently avoids discussing important issues or is unwilling to share their thoughts and feelings, it could indicate deeper problems in the relationship. Communication is essential for resolving conflicts and building intimacy. A persistent lack of communication can lead to misunderstandings, unresolved issues, and emotional distance.

Disrespect: This can manifest as belittling comments, ignoring your boundaries, or making you feel inferior. Respect is fundamental for any healthy relationship. When a partner disrespects you, it undermines your self-worth and the foundation of mutual respect needed for a strong connection.

Jealousy and Possessiveness: While a little jealousy is normal, extreme jealousy and possessiveness can lead to controlling behavior and emotional abuse. This behavior often stems from insecurity and can restrict your freedom, leading to a toxic and suffocating environment.

Inconsistency: When a partner's behavior, words, or actions are unpredictable or contradictory, it can create confusion and mistrust. Consistency is key to building trust; without it, you may constantly feel on edge, unsure of what to expect.

Avoidance of Responsibility: If your partner consistently avoids taking responsibility for their actions or blames others for their problems, it can be a sign of immaturity or a lack of accountability. A healthy relationship requires both partners to own their actions and work together to resolve issues.

Dishonesty: Frequent lying or hiding information is a significant red flag undermining trust and transparency. Trust is the cornerstone of any relationship, and dishonesty can erode this foundation, leading to suspicion and resentment.

Isolation: If your partner tries to isolate you from friends and family, it can indicate a controlling and manipulative personality. Isolation tactics can make you dependent on your partner for support, making it harder to leave an unhealthy relationship.

Emotional Unavailability: A partner who is emotionally distant or unavailable may be unable to provide the support and connection needed for a healthy relationship. Emotional unavailability can lead to loneliness and frustration as you struggle to connect more deeply.

Excessive Criticism: Constantly criticizing or finding faults in everything you do can damage your self-esteem and create a toxic environment. Constructive criticism is healthy, but excessive negativity can make you feel inadequate and demoralized.

Aggression: Any form of physical or verbal aggression is a major red flag and should not be tolerated. Aggression can escalate into abuse and pose a serious threat to your safety and well-being.

Trusting and Acting on Your Intuition

Your intuition is a powerful tool in recognizing red flags. If something feels off, trust that feeling and take it seriously. Intuition often picks up on subtle cues that your conscious mind may overlook. Acting on your intuition involves having the courage to address concerns directly and making decisions that protect your well-being. Here are some techniques for early detection of unhealthy patterns:

Observe Behavior: Pay close attention to how your partner behaves in different situations, especially under stress or conflict. Consistent negative patterns are a cause for concern. Notice how they treat others, such as friends, family, and even strangers, as this can provide insights into their character.

Communicate Openly: Have open and honest conversations about your concerns. Observe how your partner responds to feedback and whether they are willing to discuss and work on issues. Effective communication can reveal a lot about their willingness to improve and grow with you.

Seek Outside Perspectives: Sometimes, an outside perspective can provide clarity. Talk to trusted friends or a therapist about your observations and concerns. They can offer objective insights and support your decision-making process.

Set Boundaries Early: Clearly define and communicate your boundaries early in the relationship. Observe whether your partner consistently respects these boundaries.

Setting boundaries helps establish mutual respect and prevents future conflicts.

Reflect on Your Feelings: Regularly check in with yourself about how you feel in the relationship. Persistent feelings of unease or discomfort should not be ignored. Trust your emotions as they can signal underlying issues that need attention.

Deal Breakers

Personal deal breakers are non-negotiable boundaries for your well-being and happiness in a relationship. These might include dishonesty, lack of respect, incompatible values, or different life goals. Clearly defining these deal breakers helps you make decisions that align with your core values and needs.

Strategies for Maintaining a Balanced and Healthy Relationship

Effective Communication Techniques

Active Listening: Fully concentrate on what your partner is saying without interrupting. This shows respect and helps in understanding their perspective. Active listening involves giving your full attention, nodding to show you are engaged, and avoiding distractions. It helps your partner feel heard and valued, strengthening your connection.

Open-Ended Questions: Ask questions that encourage your partner to share their thoughts and feelings in depth. Instead of yes or no questions, use phrases like "How do you feel about...?" or "What do you think about...?" This invites a deeper conversation and helps you understand your partner better.

Non-Verbal Cues: Pay attention to body language and facial expressions to understand the full context of the conversation. Non-verbal cues can reveal a lot about how your partner is feeling. Maintaining eye contact, observing their posture, and noticing their facial expressions can help you gauge their emotions and respond appropriately.

Reflective Listening: Paraphrase what your partner has said to show that you understand and are engaged. This involves repeating back what you've heard in your own words. It confirms that you are listening and provides an opportunity for clarification if needed.

Stay Calm and Patient: Maintain a calm demeanor during discussions, especially when addressing sensitive topics. Taking deep breaths, staying composed, and being patient can prevent arguments from escalating. This calm approach allows for more constructive and meaningful conversations.

Shared Activities

Participating in activities together can significantly strengthen your bond and create lasting memories. Whether you cook a meal, go on a hike, or work on a project, these experiences foster teamwork and mutual enjoyment. Spending time together in these ways builds a sense of partnership and support that deepens your connection. These moments often lead to laughter, personal growth, and a stronger relationship.

Shared interests and hobbies are instrumental in deepening your connection. Discover activities that you both find joy in, as they offer opportunities for shared experiences and personal growth. Trying new things, like a dance class, gardening, or traveling to new places, injects excitement and novelty into your relationship. When you both share a passion, it not only brings you closer but also fosters mutual growth, keeping your relationship vibrant and dynamic.

Regular quality time is essential for maintaining intimacy and connection. Set aside time for activities you both love, whether it's a weekly date night, a weekend getaway, or a cozy evening at home. Prioritizing these moments reinforces your commitment to each other and ensures you stay connected, even in the midst of busy schedules. Making time for each other nurtures a strong emotional bond and creates new memories, helping the relationship remain fresh and engaging.

Tips for Staying True to Oneself While in a Relationship

Staying true to yourself in a relationship is about cherishing your personal growth while sharing your life with someone special. Think about those passions that light you up—whether it's setting personal goals, learning something new, or diving into a hobby you love. These pursuits keep you vibrant and fulfilled and bring fresh energy into your relationship. And when you support your partner's dreams, cheering them on and celebrating their achievements, you create a beautiful space where both of you can flourish. Imagine the joy of knowing that you're both growing, not just as a couple but as individuals, too.

Keeping that connection strong requires regular self-reflection and open, honest communication. Take a moment to tune into your emotions and ensure that your values, goals, and boundaries are guiding your actions. Have you talked with your partner about what's important to each of you? Setting shared goals—like planning a health routine together or exploring new adventures—brings you closer while keeping your relationship dynamic and exciting. These heart-to-heart conversations help you stay in sync, making sure you're both moving forward together, hand in hand.

As life brings changes, staying flexible and open to adjustment is key. Relationships evolve, and it's important to regularly check how your shared dreams and values align. Maybe it's time to revisit your priorities or discover new ways to support each other's growth. By staying adaptable and deeply connected, you ensure that your relationship remains strong, vibrant, and full of love. In the end, staying true to yourself while supporting your partner creates a partnership where both of you can thrive, deeply connected and ever-growing together.

Chapter 10: Legacy and Influence

"The only limit to our realization of tomorrow will be our doubts of today." – Franklin D. Roosevelt.

Impacting Others

When you share your personal stories of rejection with vulnerability and authenticity, you're not just telling a story—you're creating a ripple effect that can touch countless lives. Have you ever thought about how your experiences, when shared openly, could help someone else feel less alone? Your courage to speak about your struggles can offer hope and comfort to those who might be in the depths of their own battles. By being honest about your journey, you're breaking down the barriers that often make rejection feel so isolating. Imagine the power of your story to create a more accepting and understanding community, where people feel safe to share their own experiences without fear of judgment.

Consider how far your impact could reach if you took your message beyond personal conversations. Writing a book, starting a blog, or even giving talks and lectures can amplify your voice and allow your story to inspire a broader audience. Think about the individuals who have turned their tales of rejection into powerful messages of hope—J.K. Rowling's journey from multiple rejections to the success of Harry Potter, or the many TED speakers who have transformed their setbacks into lessons that resonate worldwide. Your story could be the catalyst that inspires someone else to keep going, to believe that there's light at the end of the tunnel, no matter how many doors have closed along the way.

But your influence doesn't have to stop at storytelling. What if you used your experiences to drive change? Imagine channeling your journey into advocacy, raising awareness about the impact of rejection, and promoting initiatives that offer support and understanding. Whether through social media campaigns, community programs, or partnerships with organizations, your voice can lead to significant change. And with your own experiences guiding you, think about the empathy and understanding you bring to those who are struggling. When you've felt the sting of rejection yourself, you're more equipped to offer genuine support and kindness to others, fostering deeper connections that can be truly transformative.

Have you ever considered the impact you could have by building or joining a community? Starting or being part of a support group—whether online or in person—can provide a lifeline for those navigating the pain of rejection. These communities become safe havens where people can share their feelings, exchange coping strategies, and lift each other up through their darkest moments. Imagine the strength and resilience that can grow from being surrounded by others who understand exactly what you're going through. In these spaces, your influence isn't just about sharing your story—it's about creating an environment where healing and growth are possible for everyone involved.

Your journey, with all its ups and downs, holds the potential to impact others in ways you might never have imagined. By embracing your vulnerability and using your experiences to foster connection, inspire action, and build supportive communities, you're not just leaving a legacy—you're creating a lasting influence that will continue to touch lives long after you've shared your story.

Mentorship

Stepping into the role of a mentor is an opportunity to make a profound impact on someone's life. As a mentor, you're not just offering advice—you're providing a lifeline of guidance, support, and encouragement to those grappling with rejection. Think about the difference you can make by being empathetic, patient, and truly listening to someone who's struggling. Your ability to create a non-judgmental space where they can express their feelings openly can be transformative. Have you ever considered how much your understanding and compassion could mean to someone at a low point in their journey? By simply being there, you're helping them see that they're not alone, and that makes all the difference.

Establishing a mentorship relationship begins with identifying individuals who could benefit from your support. Whether through professional networks, community groups, or online platforms, countless people could use your wisdom and experience. Once you've connected with potential mentees, it's important to set clear boundaries to ensure the relationship is mutually respectful and beneficial. Building trust is key—be consistent, reliable, and open in your communications. Imagine the strength of a relationship built on trust, where your mentees feel safe to share their struggles and seek your guidance without fear of judgment.

Offering guidance goes beyond sharing advice—it's about empowering your mentees to navigate their challenges with resilience. Share the coping mechanisms that have worked for you or others, providing constructive feedback that helps them improve without feeling discouraged. Assist them in setting realistic goals, breaking down larger aspirations into manageable steps. Can you picture the sense of empowerment they'll feel as they achieve these milestones? Help them see rejection not as a dead end, but as a stepping stone to growth and learning. Encourage them to reflect on each experience, teaching them that setbacks are temporary and surmountable, and that every challenge they face is an opportunity to become stronger.

And as they progress, celebrate their achievements with them. Recognize the hard work and effort they've put in, no matter how small the milestones may seem. Your acknowledgment can boost their confidence and reinforce their positive steps. Think about how motivating it is to have someone cheer you on and know that someone believes in your potential. By celebrating their successes, you're not just recognizing their achievements—you're fueling their drive to keep pushing towards their goals, and that's the kind of encouragement that can change lives.

As a mentor, you have the power to shape someone's path, help them see their own strength, and guide them toward a brighter future. It's a responsibility and a privilege that can leave a lasting impact on both your life and theirs.

Conclusion

Congratulations on reaching the end of this transformative journey! You've taken significant steps toward understanding and healing from rejection, and that's truly commendable. Have you noticed how much you've grown? Reflecting on your progress, can you see the strength and resilience you've built? You've equipped yourself with valuable tools to reclaim your self-esteem and confidently navigate future challenges. Keep this momentum going and celebrate each victory, no matter how small.

Throughout this book, we explored the complex nature of rejection, examining its emotional and physical impacts. We've discussed practical strategies to cope with rejection, from recognizing and validating your feelings to building a resilient mindset. Each chapter provided insights and techniques to help you heal, grow, and thrive. Reflecting on these concepts, have you started to implement any of the strategies in your daily life? How have they impacted your well-being? Remember, the healing journey is ongoing, and each step you take is a testament to your courage and strength.

I want to personally **thank you** for taking this journey with me. Healing from rejection and rebuilding self-worth is not easy, but your commitment to this process shows your incredible strength. Every setback is a setup for a comeback. Keep pushing forward, celebrate your progress, and never lose sight of your intrinsic value. Your journey is unique, and your resilience will inspire others. Believe in yourself, and continue to grow, heal, and thrive.

Healing and personal growth are lifelong journeys. Embrace the continuous process of learning and self-improvement. Each experience, whether positive or negative, contributes to your growth and resilience. Stay committed to your personal development, and always prioritize your well-being. Your story is a powerful testament to the human spirit's capacity to overcome and flourish.

As you continue on this path, I want to personally share with you that this book is just one **part of a series** I've dedicated to personal growth and mental well-being. In the upcoming books, I'll be diving into **mental health challenges** like depression, anxiety, and more. These resources are designed to give you even more tools and insights to support your journey. I encourage you to explore these future books as they become available, so you can keep expanding your knowledge and resilience.

If you found value in this book, I would be deeply grateful if you could leave a **"positive review on Amazon"**. Your feedback not only supports me as an author but also inspires others on their journey to healing and growth.

Remember, the journey doesn't end here. Keep striving, keep learning, and keep believing in your ability to thrive. Your future is bright, and your potential is limitless. Thank you for allowing me to be a part of your journey.

Resources and Further Reading

Recommended Books, Articles, and Websites for Additional Support.

Books

- "The Gifts of Imperfection" by Brené Brown: Learn how to embrace your flaws and live authentically.
- "Rising Strong" by Brené Brown: Discover how to get back up after falling and turn setbacks into comebacks.
- "Self-Compassion: The Proven Power of Being Kind to Yourself" by Kristin Neff: Understand the importance of self-kindness and how it can transform your life.

Articles

- Explore articles on **Mindful.org** for tips on practicing mindfulness in everyday life.
- **Verywell Mind** offers a range of articles on mental health, self-esteem, and personal growth.

Websites

- Psychology Today: Find therapists, read articles, and get advice on various mental health topics.

- Mindful.org: Resources for mindfulness practices and meditation.
- Verywell Mind: Comprehensive information on mental health and well-being.

List of Support Groups and Therapy Options

- **Meetup.com:** Find local support groups and meetups in your area.
- **BetterHelp:** Access professional counseling from the comfort of your home.
- **Talkspace:** Online therapy with licensed therapists, available through text, video, and audio messages.

Printed in Great Britain
by Amazon